# RHYTHM
# & FIRE

*W/ you in the journey,*

*—willy*

EXPERIENCING THE HOLY
IN COMMUNITY AND SOLITUDE

# RHYTHM
# & FIRE

EDITED BY JERRY P. HAAS AND CYNTHIA LANGSTON KIRK

UPPER
ROOM BOOKS®
NASHVILLE

RHYTHM & FIRE
*Experiencing the Holy in Community and Solitude*
Copyright © 2008 by Upper Room Books®
All rights reserved.

Cover design: Left Coast Design, Portland, Oregon
Cover image and part pages: *Elijah Taken Up to Heaven* by Dr. He Qi
(www.hequigallery.com)
First printing: 2008

LIBRARY OF CONGRESS CATALOGING-IN-PUBLICATION DATA
Rhythm and fire: experiencing the holy in community and solitude / editors, Jerry P. Haas, Cynthia Langston Kirk.
    p. cm.
    Includes bibliographical references.
    ISBN 978-0-8358-9964-2
  1. Spiritual life—Christianity. 2. Christian life. I. Haas, Jerry P. II. Kirk, Cynthia Langston.
    BV4501.3.R47 2008
    248—dc22

2008010953

Printed in the United States of America

For

*Danny E. Morris*

In appreciation
for his vision and perseverance
in founding
The Academy for Spiritual Formation®


And for

*all the other saints*

who journeyed with Danny
in creating this unique ministry


And for

*the members of Academy #25*

who supported the development of this book
with their prayers and financial support

# Contents

## LISTENING TO THE SILENCE

## MOVING TO THE RHYTHM OF GRACE

## LIVING COMMUNITY/LIVING FLAMES

## RADIATING FAITH

# Foreword

> They devoted themselves to the apostles' teaching and fellowship, to the breaking of bread and the prayers.
>
> —Acts 2:42

IT DOESN'T HAPPEN MUCH anymore, this kind of devotion to study, community, healthy living, and prayer. But it seems to have been the norm for the early converts to the Christian faith; and it led to a remarkable witness, as the incarnate God was reborn in those early disciples.

The frenzied lifestyle promoted and practiced by many cultures has not been able to put out the flame of desire for a better way. There continues to be a deep yearning for that kind of living and witness today that seemed such a natural part of the early Christian experience.

The way of living promoted in many parts of the world has led to a violent, anxious, divisive, and destructive environment for most who are caught up in its embrace. The peaceful, harmonious, and fulfilling life that Jesus promised seems more illusive and distant than ever. Is there a way out of the life-robbing embrace of culture that can free us for a life-giving way of living? Is there a way of living that sustains and nurtures the very best in humankind? Is there a life-giving way that ordinary people in everyday circumstances can practice?

This reality and these unanswered questions fostered the hope and dream of the Academy for Spiritual Formation nearly three decades ago. The culture's destructive ways have changed little in the intervening years. But the Academy has become an oasis of God's sustaining grace for all who, through its ministry, have sought a better, more faithful, and fulfilling way of living.

Twenty-five years later that oasis reveals itself in dozens of life-giving springs that satisfy the deep and native thirst for God that all of God's children carry within. The Academy in its many expressions continues to provide settings where thirsty seekers are immersed in the palpable presence of God and learn how to live in that presence in the daily activities of their lives.

The wisdom of the design, curriculum, worship, rhythm of daily life, emphasis on holy and holistic living, and the selection of leadership was no accident. Rather, it resulted from a several-years-long experiment in disciplined discernment, carefully and prayerfully designed and directed by Danny Morris. He gathered around him faithful seekers with a rich variety of backgrounds, skills, and experiences. Each person selected was engaged in an intentional, intense, and intimate spiritual journey. Collectively they became both a reflection of Acts 2:42 and a model of what was to come in the Academy.

The fruits of that discernment are visible in many ways including the seismic shift in the understanding, teaching, and practice of spiritual formation. This clearly ecumenical shift reaches from graduate school to Sunday school where spiritual formation is accepted and embraced as a necessary part of any curriculum that seeks to prepare followers of Jesus to live fully and faithfully as disciples and leaders.

A way of living that is faithful to the risen Christ and sustainable in the present world is as illusive and needed today as it was at the Academy's formation twenty-five years ago. The good news is that now hundreds of people bear faithful witness to the truth that a life of integrity and fidelity to God is possible in our world and that the Academy, under the leadership of Jerry Haas, continues to be that oasis where people come to drink, eat, rest—and return to live as vessels of God's saving and sustaining grace.

The spiritual journeys shared on the following pages reflect what has been sacred and life-giving, as well as visions—still forming—of what is yet to be born.

—Rueben P. Job
January 2008

# Introduction

IN THE FRENETIC VELOCITY and clanging chaos of our days, we cannot easily decipher which way to turn for wisdom and hope. Bodies are fatigued, and souls are searching. Easy answers and quick fixes, however appealing, prove inadequate for our complex world.

Every human being craves to know something, someone Greater. We ache to know home in the deepest sense. It is as if we walk through life with surroundings dimly lit or pitch black. We often stumble or lose our way not knowing where to find illumination or wondering if such a source exists.

We long for a bit of fire, as on the day called Pentecost, that will refine our spirits and energize our lives. Even as we search for answers, what we desire most is meaning that enlivens and energizes each interaction and choice.

Yet where can we turn? Self-help books, no matter how insightful, are insufficient. Where can we find a safe place to be vulnerable? How can we carve out time to experience and absorb full-souled, full-bodied rhythms in the midst of our disconnected, high-speed schedules?

Our ancestors gathered around fires and shared their life stories. By those lights, they saw one another's faces in the glow, were warmed by the experience, and came to know rhythms of giving and receiving, speaking and discerning, wrestling and resting, lament and praise.

Ancient people declared that they had heard the Creator's voice from the fire. They witnessed such startling events as God's speaking to a person and that person's continuing to live! (See Deuteronomy 5). That is the fire explored in this book, not something you or I can create with two sticks and a piece of flint or gasoline and a match. This fire, this power, this passion emanates from and is the Holy One.

The stories, prayers, and poems of people in this book make it evident that a person can live after close encounters with God—but not in the same manner. To recognize God's voice out of the fire is to come face-to-face with transformation. It is to be propelled into new life with the assurance that it is not a solo excursion.

Each writer in this book has gathered around the Fire; each one has seen the Fire in the faces of those who have encountered the living God. They write from this passion within, giving voice to the longings, fears, and experiences of life that are similar to yours and mine. Their openness, combined with their engagement in seeking, praying, serving, grappling with, and pondering Holy Mystery in community and times of solitude, equip them to be companions, even mentors, on our journeys. I invite you to open your heart as you read each rich offering. Come with your suspicions, hungers, and questions. Come experience the rhythm and be warmed by the Fire.

—CYNTHIA LANGSTON KIRK

# AWAKENING
# TO SACRED
# FIRE

# God of the Storm

Storm is coming
  I can smell it
    Watch the sky
      Glorious moment
        Power-filled drama . . .
       Coming.

Sky splits open
  Lightning strikes the eye
    Thunder rumbles, grumbles, roars.

Watch the wonder
  Spellbound by the display
Listen awestruck
  Breathing deep and free.

Smell the danger
  Count the closeness
    Hear the searing—
      Muscles tighten.

Lightning touches tombstone
  Thunder louder than imagination.

Sense the Spirit's surging shock
  Feel the resurrection.

—Jo Hoover

# Let My Prayer Be Counted

"Let my prayer be counted as incense" (Psalm 141:2).

IN THE 1950s AND '60s, Martins Ferry, Ohio, was known primarily for steel mills and coal mines. Driving along the Ohio River on State Route 7 after dark was like entering Dante's Inferno. Smoke, fire, and cinders belched from the towering smokestacks. My father would tell me of young men being rejected for military service because of cloudy spots on their lungs. The doctors thought it was TB, but it was the residue from years of breathing the polluted air.

Another industry of note in Martins Ferry was a factory that constructed wooden pallets. I was in elementary school when the box factory burned to the ground. The stacks of lumber smoldered and smoked for weeks. A thick, acrid pall hung over the south side of town as firefighters watched around the clock to make sure nothing reignited.

My twin brother and I had firm instructions from our mother, "Stay away from the box factory. You'll just get in the way!" One Saturday morning we told Mom we were going to play basketball. Instead, we walked the half-mile or so to the smoldering heap of lumber.

Scores of people circled the site as local news personalities interviewed the firefighters and the residents of neighboring houses that were miraculously spared damage. Excitement was a rare commodity in Martins Ferry, and we wanted to make the most of it. As promised, we arrived home in plenty of time for lunch, basketball in hand. Any idea that we could fool Mom quickly vanished as she pronounced, "You reek of smoke." And we did.

In her book *Wisdom Distilled from the Daily*, Joan Chittister writes of the incense that fills the monastery chapel during the Sunday vigils and the great feasts as the community prays. "What was all that incense about?" she asks and then replies:

The incense that drenches the community in a filmy heaviness once a week is another kind of reminder of the other-sidedness of prayer. Prayer, the incense says, is not an exercise in recitation. Prayer is the filter through which we view our worlds. Prayer provokes us to see the life around us in fresh, new ways. Prayer is what is left of life after the incense has disappeared.[1]

As incense rises and fills a room, be it monastery chapel or prayer closet, *everything remains the same*. All that was present before prayer remains present during prayer—friends remain friends; enemies remain enemies; problems remain problems. At the same time, however, it seems equally accurate to affirm that, as incense rises and fills a room, *everything changes*. Friends, enemies, and problems are viewed through the incense of prayer.

Some say that prayer changes things, though I cannot confess ever having had such an experience. Others say that prayer changes the pray-er. I can affirm that, though the nature of the change often eludes my ability to identify it. For me, the change wrought by prayer has been more mystery than mastery. As I have pondered the mystery of prayer in my life and as I have tried to understand the change it nurtures, it seems to me that more often than not prayer changes the way I see things. Like incense filling a chapel or a closet, prayer changes nothing except how everything else looks through its "filmy heaviness."[2]

As I read Chittister and reflected on incense as an image of prayer, I found myself wondering: Can the residue of the incense of prayer permeate the very pores of my physical body, just as the smoke from Martins Ferry's steel mills clouded people's lungs? Can the scent of a prayerful life cling to my skin and clothes, just as the smoke from Martins Ferry's box factory fire had clung to me? When I leave my times of corporate and personal prayer, do I carry the lingering scent of prayer with me? Is it possible that others discern something different about me when I've been praying? Might the prayerful residue that clings to me be transmitted to those around me? Do I see my world differently, as through the incense of prayer? Does my prayer count as incense?

—BOB MITCHELL

# Kindling the Gift

Did you ever try to make fire
when you were young
two twigs together
sliding one across the other
rapid fire
hoping for ignition
that never came

Did anyone teach you
when you were twelve
on a field trip
how fire was really made

Two sticks
one prone and pierced
the other sharp and spinning
this direction then that
burrowing its needle tip
into the fleshy wood of the other
scraps of dried grass and dead
moss thrown into the mix

Did you see it
the blue snap
eyelash-thin sparking
through a strand of moss
like electric litmus paper
the neon flame a tentative quiver
then leaping bold toward its neighbors
setting them on fire

How did the Gift come to you

When did Jesus ignite
between your twiggy fingers
When did God-fire burn your throat
choking out words
settling in the hollow pit of you
like radioactive dye
leaving you aglow
even when the world is dark

Do you remember the spirit fire
how it charred away your old self
how it burst open the seeds
of the long dormant life at your core
the blue inferno searing into your brain
a vision of the possible

Do you understand—
You're the burnt offering

Deliver the God-sparked Jesus-flamed
Spirit-fired whole and human
divinely flawed and made perfect
burning bush of you
straight into the arms
of this parched and arid world
this tinder dry world waiting to be engulfed
by the wildfire that is God

Then, in your ash and ember voice
speak to those who would be kindling
preach to those who would be fuel
and tell them this—
I bring you life.

—CATHY WARNER

# Carved in the Palm of My Hand

ANDREA BOCELLI'S powerful voice filled my study as I responded to the strains of "Tremo E T'amo," my legs and arms remembering the graceful movements of my youth when I studied dance. As my offering to God, I began to pray using only my body as the instrument of communion. Bocelli's voice sang words I did not understand; but lost in the music, I moved with abandon, desiring only that the worship be pleasing to my Lord. As the song swelled to completion, both arms lifted in the posture of the Crucifixion and in perfect timing with the final note of the work, my head bowed and breath sighed out from me. The faces of six youths who sexually assaulted me when I was thirteen appeared in my mind's eye at the precise moment God whispered, "Nancy, can you forgive them yet?"

Staggered by the question, the words hung suspended between us for what seemed like forever. I clutched my stomach in the waiting silence and gasped for breath as if I had just been hit square in the gut. "Oh . . . Oh, God. . . . Oh, dear God, I don't know," was all I could manage as I made my way to a chair near the window. But I knew in my center that I must stay with the invitation. Legs suddenly weak, I sat down hard, breathing deeply to calm myself. Aware that I could approach this almost intolerable question only if given to see what God was doing as those boys violated my body, I asked the Lord to go back to the moment of the attack twenty-nine years earlier.

Closing my eyes, I remembered the place, its darkness . . . the countless hands, the betrayal, the incredulity, the impotence, the shock, the pain . . . the terrible shame. And then I saw him. In the very moment when I experienced myself as utterly abandoned to evil and the destruction of all the hope a young woman carries in her body, in that very moment I saw him. Jesus was kneeling beside my body as it lay on the ground in the snow, jacket off, clothing torn and in disarray while the boys invaded me. His body was oriented toward me, turned toward my head; but his face, streaming with tears, was averted. Jesus was staring fixedly at his hand held out before me to see. The intensity of his gaze drew my own to it, and there, in the midst of this colossal violation, I was shown my heart . . . held in the palm of his hand. And that heart was beautiful and whole and absolutely unsullied!

In that blessed moment, I was given to know in the depths of my soul that those boys had not damaged me as much as I had always believed; that despite the sin of what went on beside the school on that frigid winter night, my core—my truest self—was then, was still, and would forever be beautiful and complete and unblemished.

Then Jesus' own words came, "They know not what they do." I remembered that the worst of the perpetrators had come from an abusive home. God did not ask me to forget. No, I was simply being asked to forgive. Finally, after all the aching years spent trying to come to terms with the goodness of human sexuality, I knew I could do what I was being asked to do, "Yes," I said. "I can forgive them now."

The moment I uttered those words, the weight of struggle and shame fell from my body; I felt light, filled to overflowing with the healing spirit of God. I sat for a long time in awe of the grace inside and around me, breathing in a kind of love indescribable. I rose after a while and went upstairs. For the first time since that shattering night, I saw a woman in the mirror who was absolutely lovely. I knew, in the center of myself, that I was free to own and celebrate my sexuality and to dance the God-given gift of it—free at last by the grace of a gracious God!

—NANCY FINLAYSON

# Remembering

In the bright morning light
Yesterday's feet form deep
Snow impressions
Along a path of Love.
Steps stretch
From hearth to woods
And back again
Gathering kindling for a fire
Unfinished. . . .

Memory fuels the heart.
Love turns the question inside out
Remember me.
Remember me.

Fox-with-No-Tail returns
(You saw him yesterday,
remember?)
crosses the path of Love
cushioned on silent snow
unmindful of dismemberment
living a tale to tell,
heir of enough.
Memory informs the heart.
Love stands the question on its head.
Remember me.
Remember me.

Memories move through snowy steps
To incense on the pillow,

Sink toward holy ground, melting
Wet with promise
And sacred tears.
Love speaks in tongues
Tasting sweetness
Tracing textures as way opens . . .
Respecting guarded corners of the soul.
Memory transforms the heart.
Love bears the question with no loss.
Remember me.
Remember me.
Christ Jesus, be
The memory of my heart.
Sanctify my brokenness
Which begs your Light and
Healing touch.
Shape my passion,
Form my living.
Walk me out of self
Along the path of Love,
Gathering kindling for a fire
Unfinished. . . .
As I remember thee,
Remember me.

—LYNDA JOAN MORLEY

# The Year from Hell;
# The Year of Grace

$\sim$

IN THE SPRING OF 2005 my daughter Laurence was diagnosed with breast cancer; my other daughter Ruthie needed heart surgery. The year from hell had begun.

Laurence went into surgery, then chemo and radiation, kicking and screaming all the way. She resisted treatment and fought every step of the process. Finally she stopped fighting the treatments and began to trust her doctors and the medical care they prescribed. She slowly moved from fear to trust, growing spiritually through the process.

Ruthie thought she was well prepared for the surgery. She meditated regularly and felt at peace before the operation. Then everything went wrong; the surgery had been successful, but the recovery nearly killed her. She ended up on the floor in my arms with blood everywhere; I thought I had lost her. After another surgery, more hospital stays, and severe anxiety attacks, she began to recover very slowly.

During Ruthie's months of recovery, I feared the worst. I thought she would die or remain an invalid living in her twilight room. I was so stressed from helping her, her husband, granddaughter, and Laurence that I could barely pray. I simply had nothing left. What a gift and grace to know that my prayer group and others were praying when I could not.

My spiritual director also helped me accept the heart wrenching illnesses of my daughters as a part of life, bringing me to say, "This is the way it is; this is the reality." I never asked, "Why is this happening to *me?*" As difficult as their illnesses, care, and facing my daughters' mortality was, I learned three things: to trust, to rest, and to receive.

I learned to trust that God would see my daughters and me through this crisis, to trust God as a presence each step of the journey so that ultimately—no matter the outcome—all would be well.

I learned the value of rest, even though I didn't do much of it. A line from Psalm 131 spoke deeply to my soul: "I have calmed and quieted my soul, like a weaned child with its mother; my soul is like the weaned child that is with me" (Ps. 131:2). I changed the words slightly and developed a breath prayer that sustained me for many months: "As a child lies quietly in its mother's arms, so may my heart be quiet within me." This prayer helped me experience physical and spiritual rest.

And I learned to receive from others: comfort, care, support, and love that enabled me to take life one day at a time. I often find myself on the giving end in life; I am thankful that I could openly receive whatever was offered and see these gifts as evidence of God's gracious and generous spirit.

I have been a spiritual director for almost twenty years, but during the worst of that year I did not see any directees. Then one day I heard God saying to me, "Jeanne, you are not their spiritual director; I am. You may feel you have nothing to give but trust in me and offer who and where you are for use by me with them." These words freed my spiritual and emotional state. I returned to my vocational task filled with God's presence and joy—another lesson in trust.

Both of my daughters are doing well. Laurence has been cancer free for over a year—wonderful news! But the best news is that she is a new and transformed person; her journey brought her to a deeper sensitivity and a grateful heart. It took Ruthie over a year to heal and regain her spark and spunk. Her experience enabled her to see every moment as God-infused. Her faith has brought her to a new place.

I am a strong woman, but my strength was no match for what I faced. Through this ordeal I came to understand that my greatest strength came in admitting that I could not handle this alone; only with God's strength and help could I make it. I have rediscovered how fragile and how precious life is, how overwhelming is the incredible love and grace of God, and how life-sustaining it is to live in the present moment. What began as the year from hell became the year of grace. Thanks be to God!

—JEANNE VARNELL

# Praying for Vision

CHRIST, MY SERVANT LORD, I seek to do your will, yet I am so often discouraged by what I see and what I know. What I experience often beats me down, driving out my joy and dreams and even the sight of you. But your faithful Spirit dwells with me, stirring my heart and my mind. And so I pray that you who are the Dreamer, the Joy, and the Hope of the Ages would sow in me dreams and visions of what is yet to be, that what is may never so fill my seeing that I am unable to see you, so conquer my knowing that I cease to know you, or so paralyze my doing that I fail to serve you. Amen.[3]

—MINERVA G. CARCAÑO

# I Wait No Longer

I wait no longer.

I waited . . . and waited more . . . for the church to step up and be a
healing partner
for the betrayal that was its own.

I wait no longer.

The body of Christ gathered in this new place has offered, by proxy, a voice
    of confession,
    of holy outrage,
    of tender compassion,
    of invitation back into right relationship.

I wait no longer.

"There can be no healing without justice."

The justice I longed for will never be accomplished.
I lay my expectation down.
Instead, this new communion of saints has become justice for me.
Not the kind of justice
    I wanted,
    hoped for,
    worked for,
    prayed for
but perhaps the only justice I can hope to see.
Whatever else, I lay my expectation down. I lay it down.

I am no longer Sister Expectation for what was.
I have been named anew. I am Sister Expectation of what will be.

I wait no longer
in sorrow.
Now, O God, I wait in hope.

—Sonja Ingebritsen

# Awakened by Sacred Fire

I HAD JUST ENTERED the front door of a beautiful house. Its layout resembled the house I lived in for the first twenty-five years of my life, yet this house was larger and more elegant. In its entry hall was a beautiful tree growing in a large round pot. Each of its three main branches was topped by healthy green leaves. They had obviously been skillfully pruned and well cared for. Their asymmetrical design was perfect for the tree's location. On its right, a staircase led up into darkness. On its left was a closed door, apparently to a hall closet. As I reached for the doorknob, my right arm brushed against one of the tree's branches. To my surprise it snapped like a brittle, dead stick might. But the broken part didn't fall off. It hung open like a hinge. The exposed surfaces were crinkly, glowing, red-orange. I realized that the whole tree was full of fire! Then I woke up.

I was spending the night at my parents' home; the previous day had been painful. I had shared with my parents some exciting new awareness to which recent reading had led me about my typical ways of functioning and theirs. I had seen that although I was nearly fifty, in many ways I still functioned like a child. To my dismay, my parents heard what I said as a rejection of all they had done for me, their only child.

As I headed for home the next morning, my parents and I were all in tears. I felt crushed by having unwittingly hurt them. But I also felt as if a huge burden had been lifted, and I couldn't forget the fire-filled tree. More than twenty years later now, I still can't.

Growing up, I'd often wondered about the dreams in Bible stories: Jacob's ladder dream and Pharaoh's dreams interpreted by Joseph. I found it very odd that these were said to be messages from God. No one I knew took dreams seriously, but I never heard anyone question these Bible stories.

As a lifelong, active churchgoer I felt similarly about quite a bit that I heard in church. A lot of it didn't make sense to me, yet I never heard anyone question it. In church, as in every other aspect of life during those years, I kept quiet and did what I was told. If something didn't make sense, I filed it away and hoped it would make sense later.

A few years before the fiery-tree dream, however, I'd begun taking some tiny steps out of that forty-year pattern. Turmoil in my church had made me angry enough to investigate the church's real purpose and why a lot of our "busyness" didn't accomplish much that mattered. I investigated by reading. I started by rereading the Bible and then moved on to various religion-related subjects and then to information about personality types, stages of faith, and depth psychology. This marathon of reading felt like a personalized, custom-designed course of study to prepare me for something, though I had no idea what that might be.

Dream work had been one topic of my reading, so when the fiery-tree dream came along I saw meaning in it. I realized that in the symbolic language of dreams, the tree depicted my life and the roles my parents and I played in it. The break in one branch symbolized the split I had just made in my lifelong way of never saying anything to my parents that I thought they would disapprove of. I remembered that in the Bible, fire had often represented God's presence; and I made a connection between the burning tree and the burning bush. Thus my dream seemed to imply that my life was full of God's fiery presence, revealed in the break I had just made. The stairs, I realized, addressed a future that I couldn't yet see. I had the sense that behind the closed door were items I needed to clean out and dispose of.

Only later did I realize that the fire also depicted anger. I'd grown up believing that nice people didn't get angry. I told myself I was not angry, but my life was full of it. I was angry about what I saw happening in the church—the passive attitude of lay members and the church's failure to address my stifled questions about scriptures that didn't make sense and about the church's real purpose.

I soon connected these two meanings of fire. God's presence was becoming apparent to me through my anger. My anger had become my God-given motivation to change from quiet conformist to needed vocal nonconformist in the church.

That motivation has led to many new steps. Early ones included participating in the newly formed Academy for Spiritual Formation and feeling like a real adult as I traveled alone to its sessions and experienced the exhilaration of its stimulating content and friendships with newly discovered kindred spirits. During my two Academy years I also attended seminary, which in my earlier years I could have never imagined doing. My new steps eventually included starting a monthly letter *Connections*, about church-related topics, which I've now been writing and publishing for fifteen years. My third book is soon to be published, and I speak to church groups throughout the US. I'm no longer keeping quiet. Now when I see the church functioning in ways that don't make sense or that seem to contradict Jesus' teaching, I speak up.

My efforts generate interest and conversation but sometimes elicit attacks and rejection. I'll continue to speak. The scene from my long-ago dream remains as clear to me as anything I've witnessed in waking life, and I'm still fanning the flame it showed me.

—Barbara Wendland

# Forging Ahead

We're all being hammered down
smashed flat, quivering red and molten
like silver in refiner's fire

We're all being punched and pushed
squashed, spun, dizzy and thrown
like clay on potter's wheel

Maybe we should've kept our mouths shut
kept our noses in our books
kept our hands in the dishwater
kept our feet on the gas pedal
kept our lives settled, stable
and possibly, doubtfully, content

But we had to do it, look up from
our circumscribed lives
remove our rose-colored glasses

pry our fingers from their death grip
around familiar's throat
and belt out those words

Melt me, mold me.

Who would've known asking for God
would be this messy, this ugly
leaving us purple and bruised
dumped into the unknown
Who would've known we're not in control

Whether we like it or not
whether we admit it or not
God always had hands all over us
fingers poking and prodding
hot breath in our faces
whispering, shouting
when we lost attention

You're mine.

So there we were and here we are
forging ahead sharpening our trust
kneading our faith

How else are we going to become silver forks
spearing meaty portions of justice for the poor?
How else are we going to become cooking pots
steaming with hope to feed the hungry?

How else are we going to rise up and follow
telling our stories of transformation
from mound of slimy clay to Communion cup,
from chunk of ore to steeple bell?

How else are we going to stare straight
into the world's face
shift our weight in the Creator's palm
and cry

Fill me, use me.

—CATHY WARNER

# Making Light

SOMETIMES I THINK DARKNESS is not a place that I feel my way through but a burden I carry in a sack. I dither about how to handle the sack, often shifting its weight to a shoulder or a hip or a crook of the arm but rarely setting it down for long.

The frayed string that holds it shut is my trick of ignoring its weight. How heavy can this be, this bagful of darkness? If darkness itself is the absence of something—the absence of light, the absence of God, or truer yet, the absence of full contact with God—then what ingredients give it weight? Insecurity, regret, jealousy, fear, and such as these amass the weight. Light is lost; fear is packed for the journey; and so it goes.

For years, these weighty things—these personal failings in faith, hope, or charity—never saw much daylight on my watch. Whining or railing had no place in holy conversation with God. Prayer required my best foot forward and both feet shod with Sunday shoes.

Years ago my high school class followed the tradition of choosing symbols to characterize itself as a community. Crystallized in my memory is the moment the class president announced our motto ("It is better to light a candle than to curse the darkness") in a schoolwide assembly. But when he stated the motto, he added one little word and shortened another: "It is better to light a candle than to curse in the dark." What a difference a tiny word like *in* can make. Our reworded motto was not so much a call to overcome darkness with light as it was an affirmation for making enough light for our cursing.

Decades have passed, and I have come to a surprising appreciation for the garbled motto. It makes uncanny sense now—both cursing the darkness and bringing curses out of the darkness into the light. Take the Psalms, for example. Day after day, the Psalms call out to me with their blessings and their curses. Psalm 139, my favorite, consists of three parts love and one part hate. The first eighteen verses celebrate God's intimate care for us, and that is where most public readings stopped. The next four verses, with their call for killing the wicked and reveling in hatred of God's enemies, always got left out of my devotional life.

Perhaps my experience is common: While growing up, my sister and I were instructed by our parents never to say we hated anything. We were not to use the word *hate*. We did not *hate* tomatoes; polite folks "did not care for" tomatoes. I did not *hate* a schoolmate who told hurtful lies; I "did not care for" what she did and never wished her ill out loud. For me, exposing my ill temper to God was beyond possibility. Keep it in the dark bag. Carry it around, no matter how heavy. Plug its holes with more dark patches.

In these new days, walking in the company of wise ones who know the desert as well as the floods, the mothers and fathers of my ongoing spiritual formation, I am beginning to see the importance of claiming full humanity in the presence of God. Can it be that God who welcomes glorious expressions of praise is also open to ugly words of despair and heartbreak, self-pity and revenge? If the curses of everyday life cannot be hidden from God, why strive to wrap them up and put them with the rest of the dark load?

The strain of trying to control what I speak to God, how vulnerable I will be, is enough to choke off a healthy prayer life. I do not care for this way of half-praying. To withhold rain is to summon drought; to neglect drought is to nurture only desert. What I want to cultivate in this dark desert is the courage to share my full self in God's presence—in the midst of blessings, in the midst of cursings, in the days of light, and in the long darkness I hang on to as if it were a treasure.

Since there is enough darkness in the world to go around, I do not need to keep a personal reserve. I am free to share with the Holy Spirit the weight of what I lack as well as the excesses that load me down. And this freedom must be candle enough to light my way to a place where I can sing a whole psalm, pray a whole prayer, and offer God my whole self as my best self.

—Linda Tatum

# LONGING
# AND
# WRESTLING

# White Tulips

On the kitchen counter
Bound by a plastic pot
They strain toward
The sunny window.
I've come for water
And the tulips startle me
With their naked longing
For light. They arch
Their long-stemmed throats,
Lean their cups
Against the panes
To catch whatever they can.
They yearn
As I yearn,
As we are meant to yearn.

—LORA MOORE

# Yearning in the Darkness

THE SUFI POET Jalal al-Din Rumi tells the story of a man whose heart-felt prayer to God is quashed by a cynic demanding proof that prayer is answered. In a dream, the shaken believer receives the deepest truth of prayer: "This longing you express is the return message."[1] The longing that underlies both grief and joy draws us into living relationship with God, quite apart from whether or not our prayer produces visible results.

There's a big market for books that tell us how to pray effectively—that is, to get the right results. Whether by following the spiritual laws of the universe or the biblical principles of intercession, the books promise to help us "get it right." While such claims may not be entirely misguided, they all have as their aim results rather than relationship, the fulfillment of our wishes rather than the refining of our desires.

More often than not, when my wife begins to lament about a problem, she's not looking to me for results. In fact, if I jump in with hardheaded, practical advice, I may run into some not-so-subtle annoyance. That's because her "prayer" to me—her yearning, desire, and unspoken request—is about relationship, not results. At such moments, she longs to be touched by some caring and love as much or more than any bright ideas I might have about solutions.

Such yearning fills the Psalms, our faith community's ancient and enduring hymnbook. Through praise-filled shouts and sorrowing sighs, fearful cries and desperate demands runs one steady current: yearning for the goodness, grace, and love of God:

As a deer longs for flowing streams,
 So my soul longs for you, O God (Psalm 42:1).

Even in times of jubilation, that note of longing is present. While the pilgrim celebrates that "our feet are standing within your gates, O

Jerusalem," his heart still yearns for "the peace of Jerusalem," beyond its recurrent wars and conflicts (Ps. 122:2, 6). Indeed, few thanksgiving psalms do not have longing and lament hidden just around the corner of some verse toward the end. Like our own hearts, these ancient hymns jam multiple emotions together in the same vessel.

Sometimes prayer does bring discernible results. We pray for guidance, and the chance word of a friend strikes us with illumination and clarity. We ask for inspiration, and an idea rises from deep within that seems to address our need. We intercede for another's healing, and the body is strengthened; or for the resolution of conflict, and our opponent seems to have a change of mind.

At other times, however, we ask, and what comes back to us is silence: "How long, O LORD? Will you hide yourself forever?" (Ps. 89:46). In such moments, the darkest moments of our lives, the only prayer possible may be our continued yearning for the light.

In the most forlorn lament of the Psalms, the sufferer complains that "forsaken among the dead" and dwelling in "regions dark and deep" he has "suffer[ed] . . . terrors" from his "youth up" (Ps. 88:5, 6, 15, BCP). Unlike other laments, this soulful cry contains no hint of anticipatory thanksgiving, no promise of praise. The ending is unflinchingly stark: "darkness is my only companion" (Ps. 88:19, BCP).

This psalm comes from a level of suffering for which there are no answers. Such a prayer is devoid of the usual upbeat reassurances of conventional faith, so much so that it may frighten the conventional believer. But it speaks the longing of those swamped by the inconsolable loss of a child or lifelong spouse, the shattered security of friendship betrayed, the irretrievable disappearance of a hope once fondly held or the dark night of clinical depression.

Even the road of intimacy with God may pass through such territory. Mother Teresa's private letters reveal that throughout the time she gave herself unstintingly to the care of the poor and dying, she suffered a sense of utter distance from the Christ to whom she had felt so close for many years before her call. Her only inner companion was darkness, a darkness she endured with faith—and a "terrible longing for God."[2] Just as Rumi affirmed, that longing itself was the sign and seal of a connection deeper than any feeling.

C. S. Lewis identified longing as the key factor in his conversion to belief in God: "that unnameable something, desire for which pierces us like a rapier" in places of beauty and haunting sounds like the "noise of falling waves."[3] He insists that any of the apparent objects of this desire is inadequate to it, because only God, the ground of our being and the goal of our longing, can satisfy it.

Our longing for health when we are sick, our aching for relationship when lonely, our desperate hoping for peace in the midst of war and for freedom when confined—even our desire for abundance when deprived and poor—all these signal a homing instinct that points us toward "the goodness of the LORD in the land of the living" (Ps. 27:13) and beyond that, for the divine itself.

Sometimes life is so difficult we can manage nothing more in our prayers than a "naked intent" toward God, a mute orientation of ourselves toward the One who is more spacious, more generous than our present cramped circumstances.[4] And sometimes that is just enough to allow us to breathe ourselves or, more accurately, be breathed back into more spacious life. Those who have been in such circumstances know that this truly astonishing gift sometimes speaks more eloquently about God's love than a shower of answers.

—ROBERT C. MORRIS

# The Gift of Tears

What is it makes me weep—in book, or film,
or gloried sky,
in church with other fragile souls,
in candle flame, in swelling song, in poignant harmony?

What is it makes me weep? The phrase
that forces breath to catch, a word
that stuns my placid mind,
feelings evoked to edge of memory.
What is it makes me weep? Hope
for so much more, much more beyond
world's drowning sorrow, violent grief,
fear's stench, convention's empty sieve.
Oh! Sweet pungent yearning for what is not,
yet must, by promise and by faith, be.

Clinging to what shines in my deep hope
I taste desire for kingdom joy,
I see with spirit eyes what mortal vision
only dreams.

What is it makes me weep? Aching beauty
of ordinary kindness,
cast of appreciative eyes,
smallest gesture of reaching love.
Oh, the imperceptible mystery of holiness
radiant in tiny acts of care.

What is it makes me weep?
The tears of grief weigh down a soul
but tears of joy buoy up the heart
with gratitude to heaven's very door.
There is so much
more.

—MARJORIE J. THOMPSON

# The Long Night of the Soul
## *A Lament for a Younger Brother*

oh what a long-long night, my dear soul
the sun has turned its face away from me
heaven's stars refuse to shine upon my face
my soul's midnight is dragging ceaselessly and mercilessly

african ancestors are refusing to bless me
heaven's angels are withholding their smile from me
cherubims and seraphs refuse me to sing along
mine is a dark, bloody, misty, cloudy, stormy, and lonely night

darkness, you have double crossed me without pity
death, be cursed—he was but so vulnerable and defenseless
hopelessness, you are culpable—you lured him into the enemy's claws
reason and logic, shame on you—you absconded at a crucial moment

who then shall hold me by the hand
in this dark-dark night of my soul?
who then shall give me a strong grip of assurance?
who then shall measure my gait and provide me with
a directional pace?

my soul hopes in no other time but morning
unlike the stubborn night, morning is compassionate
unlike the hurting night, morning specializes in healing
morning will embrace my soul and envelop it with everlasting peace

surely morning will come my way
for it was on Calvary that my Lord crushed death
surely morning shall embrace me
for it was by the apostle that death stingless and powerless was declared

death, I join the company of heaven
where is your sting? where is your power?
death, I join the saintly rebels against you
you will not rob me of a brother and still take away my hope and faith

night, you have robbed me of a brother
but morning will bestow on me his memory forever to cherish
night, with evil you have won but only the battle
but morning, with you and my Lord we have won the entire war

—R. SIDWELL MOKGOTHU

# Prayer for Comfort

GRANDMOTHER GOD, in this hour of pain we cling to you. Pulling ourselves up on your robe, we long for comfort. Place us up on your lap that we might lean our heads against your breast and feel your gentle arms around us. In times of pain, we have no solace except in you. Be with us in this dark hour. Hold us until the pain subsides.

Grandfather God, your strong yet gentle touch reassures us of safety and acceptance. Sitting with you on the porch of life and watching the beauty of your creation is a wonder beyond all wonders. Guide our eyes to catch the moments of your continued creating as your love pours out in affection and beauty. Teach us to live in your creative image.

God our Mother, when all others leave us, you remain. We stand on your promise that you will never leave us nor forsake us. Become real to us now that we will not feel orphaned but will experience your abiding presence. In Christ's name we pray. Amen.

—MARION JACKSON

# A Journey toward Home

THE HOMECOMING JOURNEY has been a dear image of my spiritual journey. I find myself in the flock of homesick cranes in the poem of Rabindranath Tagore:

> Like a flock of homesick cranes flying night and day back to their mountain nests let all my life take its voyage to its eternal home in one salutation to thee.[5]

I have been one such homesick crane since I left my home and family to come to the United States twenty-six years ago. It took a wilderness journey with many people for me to realize that my homesickness is more than a longing to be at home in Korea. My inner heart's longing and groaning desire is also to find home where I am surrounded by God's peace, joy, and love.

With a yearning heart to be closer to God, I began a courageous two-year adventure. Faithfully, I read the recommended books and participated in the eight weeks of retreat life that included daily prayer, Eucharist, lectures, silence, reflection, group sharing, and covenant group. The blessing and beauty of the journey were the forty-four companions who came from different life paths. Walking with such companions brought comfort and encouragement as well as the challenge to be vulnerable and open. It brought, in the form of a covenant group, a sacred and safe space where I felt accepted for who I was. I discovered that there was no right or wrong way to walk. Just being on the path together, being present with one another, was sufficient.

My journey those two years was like walking through a labyrinth, an ancient spiritual tool, a prayer path. I left busy activities and concerns behind me as if I took off my old shoes and my old self to enter the path, trusting the well-designed course would take me home. And

I expected that it would guide me to a center where I would encounter God. I anticipated that such an encounter would bring me to spiritual maturity; I would be more like Jesus.

Sometimes I experienced being very close to the center only to discover that I was being led out toward the outside, farther and farther from the center. I wondered if I could ever reach the center where God was. Over time I realized that the purpose of the journey was not simply reaching the center but walking on the path faithfully and patiently. As I walked, I learned to listen to my heart and to let go of things. As I walked, I reflected on my feelings and memories, including joy and hurts.

When I finally reached the center, I discovered my true self and false self. At the center, my eyes and heart opened to see the part of me that had been waiting for attention and nurture. I heard my inner voice with a listening heart. I came to my senses.

Walking out from the center of the labyrinth toward the exit, from the midpoint of the two years to the final gathering, seemed faster. As I put on the old shoes and stood there for a while, my heart was filled with joy and gratitude for completing the path. But the longer I stood, the more disturbed my heart as I pondered my spiritual maturity. I realized that I walked out to stand at the same place where I started two years previously. I was not quite as transformed as I had expected and hoped in the beginning. If I am in the same place, how have all the struggles, reflections, studies, prayers changed me?

A line from a poem by T. S. Eliot was given to me as God's gift at the moment. He writes, "Home is where one starts from" in his poem "East Coker."[6] He reminds us that only as we venture out and return do we "arrive where we started and know the place for the first time."[7]

I arrived where I started but knew the place for the first time. The place was home. Home had been with me all along. I was like the prodigal son's older brother who remained at home—but was lost at home. My ears opened to hear God saying, "In-sook, you are always with me and all that is mine is yours." (See Luke 15:31.)

We are always on our way home. Joyce Rupp describes it this way:

The more we set our hearts on this God, the more our hearts will yearn and long for a place with God. The homesick crane in us will deepen in intensity and clarity and will give us the determination and the freedom we need to keep winging our way homeward.[8]

—IN-SOOK HWANG

# A Psalm, a Longing

IT GRABBED HOLD OF ME and wouldn't let go—a strange thing to say about a Bible passage, but that's what happened. Psalm 63 reached out and laid hold of me. For the longest time, it named and marked a particular segment of my spiritual journey. The psalm was telling me to pay attention to my deep longing.

"You are my God, I long for you from early in the morning. My whole being desires you like a dry, worn, waterless land. My soul thirsts for you" (Ps. 63:1).[9] The psalmist was singing my lines. I longed for a closer relationship with God; I thirsted for a sense of God's nearness.

The longing led me to a sabbatical year, living with Quakers in Pendle Hill, a study center outside of Philadelphia. There I learned to befriend silence, to focus on listening to God who often speaks in the "still small voice." Sitting in silence in the daily meetings for worship opened me to the depths of yearning: "In the sanctuary let me see how mighty are your works" (Ps. 63:2). I began to glimpse the deep love that God has for me.

Still, the ache and longing persisted. I was stuck in the waterless land and the thirst expressed in the opening verses of Psalm 63. I feared leaving the Quaker community and trying to develop a regular pattern of morning prayer. On my own, I had never been successful. Yet Psalm 63 had nudged a longing and a desire.

Imagine my surprise and comfort to discover Psalm 63 as part of the morning prayer pattern at the next long retreat I attended after completing my sabbatical year with the Quakers. Every morning we sang Psalm 63; its melody heightened my longing and opened me to verses beyond that poignant longing. The chanting of the verses led me to a God whose love is "better than life itself," who has always been my "constant help." It gradually dawned on me that my great longing for God was surpassed by the longing of God for me.

Howard Thurman once wrote, "With sustained excitement, I recall what, in my own urgency, I had forgotten: God is seeking me. Blessed remembrance! God is seeking me. Wonderful assurance. God is seeking me."[10] How could I have forgotten? Yet often our focus on our own needs blinds us to the signs of God's love and presence around us. God tries to get our attention in hundreds of ways, seeking to make a home in us.

I began to sense a shift when singing Psalm 63. My longing was now joined by wholehearted thanks and praise—gratitude for each new day, for the psalms, and for God who drew me into relationship with another retreat group of pilgrims and seekers. I began to move from simply longing for God to discovering ways to pay attention to God's activity in my life.

Even more, I discovered that God not only longs for me, but God aches for the whole world. God's longing is wider and deeper than my individual quest. It echoes throughout history and all of creation as well as in every heart. This knowledge led me to write the following lines of a prayer: "God, you ache every time we destroy beauty, every time we harm one another, every time we ignore the outstretched hand and turn away from the poor and wounded. . . . You call us to care for each other, to give up our greedy habits and our violent ways."

I still love to sing Psalm 63 from the *Upper Room Worshipbook*, though I don't need the words or the book anymore. I know the melody and lyrics and have internalized the message and wisdom. Psalm 63 remains a dear friend and companion of many years, naming my longing and guiding me to the source and fulfillment.

—LARRY PEACOCK

# Psalm Prayer (Ps. 34)

In your compassion, gracious God,
   you hear the cry of the poor, the needy, and the lonely ones.
May we also hear the cries of our brothers and sisters,
   responding in love as you have shown us in your Son,
   our Savior, Jesus Christ. Amen.[11]

—ELISE S. ESLINGER

# Psalm Prayer (Ps. 91)

O God, you are our refuge and deliverer.
When we are wounded or ill you send angels—
    human and divine—to minister to us.
Through Christ we are bound to you in love
    our whole life through.
And, we dwell secure in the shadow of the Most High.
Thanks be to God. Amen.[12]

—GINGER HOWL

# God's Glimmer on *O Sapienta*

Even the darkness is not dark to you;
　the night is as bright as the day,
　for darkness is as light to you.
　　　　　　　　　　　—Psalm 139:12

I READ THE PAPERS each day. I read the reports of wars both great and small. I read where again today there were bombings of someone's fathers and mothers and sons and daughters somewhere. I read the papers, and I long for peace. I would settle for truce most days or even an informal cessation of hostilities.

I read the stories of random and not-so-random violence and am stunned by what we are capable of doing to each other, what we do in the name of everything from greed to God.

I listen to the world around me each day. I listen as the general tone of discourse about anything of value and anyone who matters —and who does not matter—grows less and less civil, less and less reasonable, less and less hopeful.

I listen as the ones who would lead us discount and mislead and disregard us, all of us, once they have taken up their places of authority. I listen to the bickering and blustering as the societies we inhabit become more and more dysfunctional and as the planet we live on comes apart at its very seams. I listen to the world, and I wonder if today there will be a single thoughtful conversation about the things that matter in the halls of power.

I look around me each day. I look with dismay, knowing that we who have much might not do much at all this day for those who have little. I watch as we do not feed those who are hungry, insure those who are vulnerable, protect those who are at risk, provide for those who are sick.

I look at what our treasure really seems to be after all and where we spend it and who we spend it on. I look around me, and I long for us to make any sacrifice at all for someone else, be it reasonable or lively or otherwise.

I walk the streets each day. I go past the houses of the elderly, the ones who are alone and afraid and hungry who hide behind their curtains and their locked doors so that no one will know. I go past the ones who have no doors to lock and no roof over their heads either, the ones who sleep in the streets where I walk. I go past young people with blank faces and sullen eyes and angry hearts, and I wonder what will become of them.

I walk the streets each day, and I long for the streets themselves to be empty of fear. I carry a kind of darkness with me everywhere now, within me and without me. It is not the darkness that You have made—the night You have given us "for the refreshment of our minds and bodies,"[13] as the old prayer calls it, the darkness you have given us for silence and rest, gifts we now squander with abandon.

I carry with me some of our self-made darkness each day. I can no longer pretend that it is not all around us and among us and within us.

I read the Ancient Story. I make my prayers. I walk the aisles of a cathedral. I listen to my own heart. I look for signs and wonders. I carry my share of our darkness. And I long for our darkness, the darkness that we make, to go away. The darkness may not be dark to You, but it is very dark to me. Each morning I sit in the remains of the dark that You gave us. It is before the sun comes. And I wait for it all to begin again. And I wait for You.

A priest who has been as much friend as priest to me tells me that the opposite of faith is not really doubt after all. The opposite of faith, he says, is certainty. Certainty is something I have very little of, if any at all. Perhaps I am certain of only one thing: I will wait for You each day, in your dark, longing for You to come and bring the light to shine in the darkness that we have made.

This waiting is an act of faith, made in the dark in the absence of certainty. Some days this single and small and unseen act of faith is all that I can muster and, perhaps, all that really matters.

Grant that we may find You and be found by You, go the words of the old prayer.[14] Indeed. Amen. So be it.

It is Advent just now as I write this. It is *O Sapienta,* the first of the eight days of prayer before the night of the Child is upon us. And so I pray. May God let there be light again, tomorrow, to take away the darkness of the night You have given us in your wisdom and mercy. And may the Light of the world come soon, to shine on us, we who live in darkness, as Zechariah has taught us to sing (Luke 1:78, 79). And may there be a glimmer of light this day, in the darkness that we ourselves make in this world, the world for whom we are to be the light. Amen. So be it.

—ROBERT BENSON

# Prayer for Mercy

GOD OF MERCY, we are in such need of your tenderness. Often unable to live fully and afraid to die, we are paralyzed by pain, incapable of holding the world's despair and our sense of impotency. We cannot bear a world without hope. We come to this crossroad, lay open our burdens and fears, and wait in silence and stillness for you. Amen.

—CHRIS BAHNSON

# Sonnet

Now the dark days of wintertime draw nigh

Life is suspended on a wisp of breath

The trees stand skeletal against the sky

and fields lie fallow, desolate with death

The flower beds that lately bragged of blue

are brown and dry beneath the blowing snow

My heart is cold and I have withered too,

as leaves descend and drift where'er winds go.

When winter comes then we should take our rest

let go the doing and learn how to be

In darkness and in barrenness we test

our willingness to trust the Mystery

'til Mystery becomes our daily bread

our light, our joy by which all life is fed.

—HAZELYN MCCOMAS

# Unexpected Guests

LOOKING BACK over all my years, I now see that I spent most of the first half of my life in a kind of darkness. I didn't have a happy childhood. I was a daydreamer, usually in trouble at home and at school for my inattention and failure to complete my work. I brooded over things like the possible death of my parents, my perception of God's rage over my struggle to make myself believe that there had been an actual Adam and Eve, as well as my fear that "they" were about to drop the atomic bomb on "us." I lived with an ongoing terror that my father was about to punish me once more for something I couldn't anticipate. Indeed, from childhood, I struggled against that wrenching yearning for something that I really could not identify.

The obscure longing did not go away after my parents divorced, even though my circumstances changed. Throughout high school, college, graduate school, and young adulthood, the darkness would envelop me at times. On other occasions, I could see a little, just a little, into that deep, dark place of stabbing desire and behold something—knowledge? beauty? goodness? love? What, for heaven's sake?

In my thirties, I felt sure I had found the answer to the question when I fell in love with Richard, and we married. The joy I felt at the sight of his curly hair, at his consistent kindness to me, by the children's delight in him and his in them filled me full. I burrowed with pleasure into the love I was sure had been the object of my desire all along.

The time came, however, when I became aware that darkness was once again deepening around me—a darkness accompanied by desperation. My awareness began on an ordinary Saturday almost thirty years ago.

It started like this. Richard had gone out early to run his usual weekend errands, and I had asked, as I always did, when he would be back. He had answered, "One o'clock." By 3:00, I was beside myself with speculations and questions. Had Richard been in an accident? Should I begin to call the hospitals? Or had he been in the grocery store and suddenly realized, between the canned tomatoes and the dried beans, that he had made a mistake to marry me? Perhaps instead, some beautiful, young girl was busy beguiling his heart away. He was, after all, my sunlight in the darkness.

The stupid thing was, there was nothing in the slightest unusual about Richard's lateness or my desperation. Richard was always late on Saturdays. He didn't mean to be; he just hadn't a clue about how long it would take him to do anything. Knowing that fact never did me any good. I worried obsessively and increasingly about the same things.

This particular weekend when things had become unbearable, I was given a gift. For years I had been teaching the spiritual traditions of ancient Christianity. The great male and female teachers, the abbas and the ammas, of Egyptian monasticism had been guides for me and many of my students as well. In the middle of Saturday afternoon while Richard was still gone, a small group of these ancient teachers dragged me from my study, so to speak, and sat me down on the living room couch for a talk.

While my stomach turned over and over, Amma Theodora got right to the point. "Of course you are miserable and afraid," she said. "Don't you realize that you have invested the whole of yourself, your well-being and your happiness in your husband?"

With a start, I understood that that is exactly what I had done. I must have looked guilty.

"No," she went on gently (these teachers are always gentle), "you haven't done anything wrong. You know that God made all things in such a way that longing and desire are at our core, but the only place we will ever find the object of our longing—and with it our true selves, our true love, our true security, our true grounding—is in God. But that fundamental longing so easily gets misplaced." Amma Theodora went on, "Of course, everything gets broken, even your love for your husband, but we try to live as though this isn't the case. Roberta, do you recall what Abba Poemen said? 'Do not give your heart to that which does not satisfy the heart.'[15] This is just what he meant."

There was a pause in the conversation while I thought about what she was saying to me. Then Abba Poemen spoke: "So, Roberta, love your husband with joy and delight. Love all the good things of your life: your whole family, your friends, your work, this beautiful world, but don't ask Richard or any part of your life to give you what they can't give. We are made to love, but you know yourself that desperation is the enemy of love. It is only as any of us are able to let go of our death grip on whomever or whatever we love that we can even see them in all their goodness for who they are and not just who they are for us."

There was more silence as I thought. Then Theodora asked, "Are you willing to try to find your center in God?"

"Yes," I answered faintly, "but I don't think I know how."

"Roberta," she said, "first give up the unrealistic expectations of yourself and be gentle with yourself. Why don't you begin with a very easy daily discipline of prayer? Remember, you are on a very long road, one you will travel your whole life. You will find deep satisfaction in many places, but at many other places you won't know what you are doing or even who God is a lot of the time. This is just the way it is with the spiritual life. But I can promise you that you too will eventually learn that what Abba Arsenius said to all of us is true: 'If we seek God, [God] will show himself to us, and if we keep [God], [God] will remain close to us.'"[16]

There was more silence as I filled up with gratitude and love. I bowed my head and said thank you to my great teachers. I trusted that they had spoken into the exact place of my darkness. I have found my life to be exactly as they said it would be. I still seek God; God still shows Godself to me in darkness and in light and, paradoxically, in all my seeking, God remains close.

—Roberta Bondi

# LISTENING
# TO THE
# SILENCE

# About Wind

It stirs up my yard. Not far
From where I weed the beans
It agitates the tops of trees.
In one a broken branch,
Upended, groans as if
It disagrees with being
Caught. Things chafe,

Things ring. The wind
Descends to sound the chimes
Hung on the porch. Five notes:
A minor scale that climbs
Into my mind, suggests
The lines of an ancient hymn:
"Let all mortal flesh keep silence."[1]

—LORA MOORE

# A Dream Door to Discernment

A HUGE SNAKE PREPARED to swallow me. So began my life-changing dream the final week of a spiritual formation retreat in 1990. Filled with fear, I made myself as skinny as possible, ready to be consumed. Even as I stood in anxious expectation, I sensed I would somehow survive this swallowing. I hadn't a clue what the dream really meant or what transformation it might be pointing me toward. Yet that dream rarely left me—it lingered in my unconscious, like a door not yet open, and left me longing for something I could not name.

In 1992, while serving full time as a campus minister at the University of Washington, I sensed a slight opening of the closed door, an inner shift calling me to a deeper place. On the surface, I bobbed along in busy and fulfilling ministry surrounded by a loving family. Below the surface, I paddled like crazy preparing to let my oldest child leave the nest and coping with the ominous beginnings of my youngest child's long and dangerous journey into addiction. Steadily, my life climbed to the upper reaches of the stress scale. My spiritual director suggested it might be wise for me to take a sabbatical. I heard her but resisted for more than a year.

One evening at a Taizé service, my dream door opened a bit more in a surprising way. As I approached the Taizé cross to pray, I received an unbidden breath prayer: "Receive me, Jesus, and take me deeper." Shaken and frightened by this prayer, I wondered what would happen if I actually began to pray it. But then I didn't really have a choice; the prayer began to rise in me before I even initiated the request.

One morning, I rose, stood at the window, and began to repeat my breath prayer. Before I had fully released my breath, I knew without doubt or fanfare: it was time for sabbatical. Though far from fully open, a thin shaft of light shone on the path from my dream door.

In February 1994 I began a year of rest and renewal, but within weeks, it became apparent to me that this sabbatical time was meant for more. Within a month, I spiraled into a painful time of facing the reality of my life and coming to terms with it. I entered therapy; went off on wilderness retreats; spent a year with a movement therapist where I learned to listen to my body (which never lies!); and learned a lot about addiction, enabling, and recovery. I was bereft as I acknowledged the wrenching letting-go process that surrounded my relationship with my addicted daughter. I felt terrified as I began to acknowledge my spouse's addiction issues and to hear God's voice calling me out of my twenty-eight-year marriage.

I rediscovered a prayer by Flora Wuellner, one she calls the "radical prayer" and began to recite it daily: "Holy Spirit, if this is right for me, let it become more firmly rooted and established in my life. If this is wrong for me, let it become less important to me, and let it be increasingly removed from my life."[2] My dream door creaked and groaned, slowly opening to admit more light.

Beneath the agony and anguish of those years, I kept hearing God asking me to choose life, to move toward the Beloved, to embrace the inner whirl of the Mystery, and to practice a ruthless trust in my process of discernment. I listened with all of my senses, reconnected with a few trusted friends, and spent hours in silence and solitude.

Then again on a very ordinary morning, my eyes flooded with tears as I acknowledged a profound sense of knowing that it was time to leave my marriage, to leave the dream of the family I had clung to for so long. God's love and assurance surrounded me in those moments, as did an awareness of a great shedding of skin that no longer fit me. My spiritual director saw me later that day and said, "It's as if you have given birth to your own soul, and God has been the midwife." This birthing process continued for quite some time and continues still, though in calmer seas these days.

The life of discernment can be a long, subtle, and painful journey. For many years my snake dream led me, holding out the elusive promise of a door opening to new life. The archetypal symbol of the snake pointed to a transformation that I could not imagine. In hindsight, I think if the door to understanding had been wide open at the time of my dream, the light would have been blinding and overwhelming—

more than I could possibly take into my being at one time. I would have ignored the invitation to dive into the depths with God. It takes time to learn to dive deep, to trust that you will not drown. It takes time to hone awareness to notice when the doors to transformation crack further open, shedding more light, spilling out more grace for the path ahead. It takes time to soak in grace and believe in the soul's beauty and goodness. It takes time to set aside expectations, attachments; let go of old patterns; embrace reality. It takes time to grieve loss and experience healing.

Being swallowed into the heart of God's abundant grace doesn't come easily to us humans! Stepping across the doorway flung fully wide and resplendent with light to receive the gifts God prepares for us takes courage, humility, perseverance, patience, trust, and the companionship of faithful friends . . . and perhaps a dream.

—SUZANNE SEATON

# Night Prayer

Final words of the day
Offered to the One
In whose image we are created.
Gratitude for a day of
Inspiration,
Guidance,
Strength,
Solace,
Splendor.
Confessing actions, inactions
Intended, unknown, ignored
When we could have chosen
To shed light on the matter.
Pleading to be kept
As the apple of God's eye
Eager to rest in holy peace.
Ancient promise of redemption
Unfolding again and forever
Like a night cereus—
Perfumed marvel to behold,
While the stars
Illuminate indigo sky
Reminding humanity
The Light is come
And no manner of darkness
Can extinguish it.

—Cynthia Langston Kirk

# Silent Listening Hearts

"WE ARE SO BUSY TALKING, God can't get a word in edgewise," a young Lutheran pastor exclaimed during a discussion on prayer. Everyone smiled and nodded in agreement, knowing from experience just what he was talking about. But as I later reflected on his comment, I recognized an inherent problem with the statement: it implied that if we fall silent in prayer, God will speak and we will hear.

That has not been my experience of keeping silent. When I am quiet, I do not hear God; I hear my chattering mind. I hear the plans I am making, the past events I am reliving, my hopes and fears about the future, and what I want to have for lunch. If I remain still long enough for my mind to eventually quiet itself, I am left in silence. No words from God, no important insights—just silence.

For many years I thought I must be doing something wrong. Maybe my earlier prayers had not been good enough. Maybe I was not listening hard enough. Then I considered that maybe God wasn't interested or didn't love me enough to speak. So I tried to perfect my verbal prayers. I changed my body positions while praying. I called on God to grant me courage and patience. I did everything I could think of to fix the silence, but only silence remained. I despaired of ever hearing a word from God.

Then one day in deep distress, I visited a friend. I poured out my heart to her, and she listened. She did not interrupt; she did not turn away. When I finished speaking, she did not tell me what to do. She simply sat with me, holding my hands and letting me know she had heard and understood. Although one part of me wished she would give me some answers, I realized her silence indicated that she loved me and trusted me to know what to do. I began to wonder if maybe this was the way God listened to me.

Another time, while I sat in companionable silence with my husband, I became aware that our love made the silence rich and comfortable. Silence with a stranger or with someone I did not trust would not be easy; I would fill the space between us with words. But with my beloved, I did not need words to recognize and celebrate our intimacy. I wondered if this might be another human model for my relationship with God.

But how could I be sure? Other people heard God when they got quiet. Were my reflections simply a rationalization for what I was not receiving? Was I fooling myself to think that God loved and trusted me so much that God did not need to speak? Could it be possible that the silence I shared with God was an assurance of our intimacy?

In the midst of my musings, I came across words of affirmation in the writings of Father Thomas Keating: "Silence is God's first language; everything else is a poor translation."[3] His words sent shivers up my spine and made my heart race. If I heard no words during silent prayer, received no images, maybe God was speaking to me in the holy language of silence. According to this wise and faithful man, God's silence could signal God's presence and love after all. I breathed a deep sigh of relief.

Later a friend told me about an interview she heard with Mother Teresa of Calcutta. The reporter had asked, "Mother, when you pray, what do you say to God?"

"I don't say anything," she replied. "I just listen."

"And what does God say?" the reporter gently prodded.

"God doesn't say anything," she responded smiling. "God just listens." I breathed another sigh of relief!

Although at times I still long to hear God's words, my struggles have eased; and I am content with the silence. As my comfort grows, I find myself listening without expectation; the silence deepens. In the quiet I listen not only with my ears but also with my heart, the marrow of my bones, and my whole skin;[4] and I imagine that God is listening to me even more intently. The holy silence of contemplative prayer has now become a celebration of the wonder of two silent listening hearts.

—JANE VENNARD

# Silence as Friend, Not Enemy

I LOVE WORDS: the sight of them on the page, the vibration of them in the air, the delicious feel of them as they roll out of my mouth, their power to describe and delight. I love water too, but I try not to forget that I can drown in it as well as delight in it. And the truth is, most of us are drowning in words.

When in a learning mode, we are particularly prone to the seduction of sound and print in all its forms—from stimulating discussions to vivid descriptions. We can become so enthralled with words that we begin to mistake the "right words" for the real thing; that is, we forget that reading a great book about prayer is not the same as praying. Words can become an end in themselves rather than a means to lead us to the experience of God. On the inner journey of spiritual formation, words can be pointers *to* God—not to be mistaken for the experience *of* God.

Our experiences of God are as varied as our faces, but one divine language enriches the growth of introverts and extroverts alike: the language of silence. The sound of silence can be both deafening and disturbing. Being still in silence can also feel like a colossal waste of time. I used to harbor secret judgmental feelings about its practitioners. After all, I reasoned, why sit mute and motionless when you could be feeding the homeless or healing the sick or doing something productive, for goodness sake? At best, I considered silent practice as one of many forms of prayer, a mere appetizer on the rich buffet of spiritual options that one could take a bite of . . . or not. Silence had to change my life before it could change my mind.

The offering of myself as an empty (but willing) container was the toughest discipline I ever tried. True silence didn't come easily for me. I viewed silence as an enemy, something to be defeated and conquered. As an extrovert who feeds on the energy of group process and conversation, I was drawn to the instant feedback of stimulating discussion, the affirming eye contact of others, and lively voices engaged in an exchange of ideas. Silence still doesn't come easy for me, but God has provided many teachers and companions along the way who helped me as a struggling novice to begin to experience, not just "know about," availability and emptiness.

The first year of practicing silence I could find no one to share this particular path in my faith journey, except my spiritual director. Someone introduced me to the practice of Centering Prayer by thrusting the instructions into my hand and leaving me alone with God. My mind wandered; my extroverted ego resisted for all it was worth. When I began to enter times of silence, I encountered voices all right, but they were strange inner voices, an unruly chorus that I came to recognize as the infamous "monkey mind," the part of us that leaps from thought to thought like a monkey swinging from tree to tree. In order to calm this inner chaos, I resorted to my usual solution to any problem: try harder. I would simply switch to effort-mode and go galloping down the path toward being a better Christian. It didn't work. It took quite a while before I realized the process was more about letting go than trying harder. I had to (gasp) release control of my spiritual growth.

Most of us begin the spiritual journey using our natural methods of unconscious control. We decide when and where to attend worship, what scriptures to read, for whom we shall pray, what inspiring speaker to listen to, and what books to read! We are accustomed to being in the driver's seat, making good decisions, and directing the journey. However, befriending the silence is

—more about yielding than controlling,

—more about loosing than grasping,

—more about participating than directing,

—more about allowing than managing.

When we submit to emptiness and silence, we take our hands off the wheel and relinquish control to the Holy Spirit. You would think we would enter that vulnerability with trust, but at first the openness makes us feel tender and naked. We may feel stripped of all pretense and the protection of words. When we aren't busy controlling and evaluating our experience, we can become simply attentive—discovering our truest selves in the mystery of silence as we learn this special language of God.

Things begin to happen, ever so slowly and subtly. As a wise mentor once told me, the silence of God is not the silence of a graveyard but the silence of a garden growing. Everything may appear dead and lifeless as we stand in the midst of a winter garden, but elementary biology tells us that bustling activity is going on underground where we can't see it or control it. Emptying ourselves, *kenosis*, and letting go of our control frees us to trust that unseen seeds, already planted by the divine, will ultimately yield the fruit of the Spirit in unexpected ways. When we finally believe and trust in this process, we can begin to befriend the silence, rather than see it as an enemy. We can trust the not-knowing and embrace the uncertainty.

Will you experience an onslaught of thought? Absolutely. Will it seem impossible to control your monkey mind? To be sure. As we still the mind, voices inside our heads compete for our attention like hummingbirds on a holiday. Our instant evaluations are often scathing; we insist that we have listened and haven't heard one single thing. Don't condemn, just notice with an inner smile; don't evaluate, just leave the timing and the harvest to God. Enter the spacious freedom found in radical trust, the freedom that doesn't have to know what's happening or when.

I'm not sure when the silence ceased to feel like an accusing enemy and became such an intimate friend, welcoming me and enfolding me in a presence and power more loving. It's become clear that I don't know nearly as much theology as I once thought I did, and I don't have nearly as many answers. But I know to whom I belong and can affirm the truth of the familiar beatitude: If we come to Christ hungry, thirsty, starving for the friendship of the divine, we shall be filled in God's sacred silence.

—LINDA DOUTY

# Prayer of Discipleship

YOU ARE THE FIRST AND THE LAST, the Alpha and the Omega; all life begins and ends in you, Lord Jesus. Why, therefore, do I struggle to be in control? Why am I in such a hurry to fill my days with things that have no eternal value? And, moreover, why do I postpone those activities that nurture the promises of eternity? Where is the passion to do your will in all things? O God, I am bold to claim the fullness of your mercy and faithfulness. I pray for the grace to submit all to you, patience to wait upon your timing, hunger for holiness, and discernment of your will. May this weak and unworthy one stand ever ready to enter the place you have already prepared, O Jesus, my resurrection.[5]

—RENÉ O. BIDEAUX

# Meditating with Tea

A FRIEND OF MINE grabs a brightly colored mug, fills it almost full with water, sprinkles some sweetener in, places a tea bag in the water, and heats it in the microwave for one and a half minutes. That is how she makes tea. She has no wasted movements, and you can tell that she has made tea in this manner many times.

We can learn much about our spiritual lives from making and drinking tea. My friend's tea-making method describes my spiritual life of many years: pressured from inside and out to succeed and be effective and do it quickly, effortlessly.

The fast pace without spiritual refreshment took its toll. In spite of being an ordained pastor, mother, and pastor's wife, part of me was dry. I was so dry that I once considered running my car into a car ahead of me so I could get some rest. Fortunately, I made time to participate in a retreat in Wisconsin—a pivotal time in my spiritual life. It reiterated much of what I already knew from the making and sharing of tea.

Recently I made tea for my tea-on-the-run friend. That preparation reminded me of many things to which God calls us: a slower rhythm at times, silence, observing life, gratitude, sharing, and relationship with God and others.

Following the custom in my home country, I gathered a bowl, a teapot, green tea leaves, and two teacups. Next, I boiled water in a teakettle for three minutes. I poured the boiling water into the bowl on the table to cool to about 175 degrees Fahrenheit.

As my friend and I waited for the water to cool, we admired the beauty of the tea set—its soft green color on which were painted delicate clouds and birds. Silently, we gave thanks for life, for our time together and other matters that came to our hearts.

I felt the outside of the bowl, checking to see if the water was the right temperature. Korean women have done this so often that it is like some mothers checking a child's temperature with a hand on the forehead. The water temperature was ready. I placed the tea leaves in the teapot and poured the hot water from the bowl into the teapot.

Casual observations and conversation are not shared during tea making and drinking. This time is given to going deeper. The one who prepares the tea begins with an observation. Others may offer observations if they choose. Silence is highly regarded. If no one speaks, people are comfortable with the silence. It is a time to reflect and pray.

"Life is water," I observed.

Silence.

"Water is essential," she said, reminding us of this precious gift.

Silence.

"Water is given to us," I stated.

Silence.

She offered, "So is life."

We experienced more silence as we reflected on spiritual matters in the deep recesses of our souls.

I poured a bit of tea into her cup and then into mine. Back and forth, I poured a bit into each cup. This way no one has weak tea and no one has tea that is much stronger. The tea is the same for all.

Silence.

When I finished pouring, I reflected, "Water flows."

Silence.

"As does God's love," she responded.

Silence.

"In the waters of baptism," I said.

Silence.

"For the waters, I am grateful," she replied.

The teatime was rich with gratitude and sharing. It was a time of paying attention to what God has done and is doing. Praise God for tea leaves that invite us into prayer and community, that offer us a pace and nourishment to refresh our souls.

—Kyunglim Shin Lee

# Losing Ourselves in Silence and Peace

O LORD, my heart is not proud
nor haughty my eyes.
I have not gone after things too great
nor marvels beyond me.

Truly I have set my soul
in silence and peace.
A weaned child on its mother's breast.
even so is my soul.
                    —Psalm 131:1-2[6]

This is an amazing statement by David.[7] How can he declare "my heart is not proud," when the scripture reminds us that "the inclination of the human heart is evil from youth" and "the heart is devious above all else"? (Gen. 8:21; Jer. 17:9). How can David claim "nor haughty my eyes," when the writer of Proverbs says, "All one's ways may be pure in one's own eyes, but the LORD weighs the spirit," and "There are those who are pure in their own eyes yet are not cleansed of their filthiness" (16:2; 30:12).

The assertion "I have not gone after things too great nor marvels beyond me" would, itself, seem to be contradicted by the previous claim of not having haughty eyes or a proud heart (Ps. 131:1). The quintessence of the fallen human condition is that we play "god" in our life. Rather than allowing God to be God in one's life on God's terms, God is either replaced by one's deification of self, or God is made subordinate to one's own agenda and self-identity. This is the essence of going after things too great and marvels beyond us. To claim perfection as David has done would seem to be the epitome of going after things too great and marvels beyond him. What on earth, then, is David saying here? His assertions suggest that he is either a fool who does not know his own condition, or he is reflecting a far deeper reality than that by which we evaluate his seemingly ludicrous claims.

The answer lies in the concluding affirmation, "Truly I have set my soul in silence and peace. A weaned child on its mother's breast, even so is my soul" (Ps. 131:2). This is the foundation upon which David makes his seemingly outlandish claims. These assertions are the consequence of an inner posture of silence and peace, a core abandonment of himself to God in love like a weaned child at its mother's breast, not a result of David's own efforts.

What does it mean, then, to set one's soul in silence? I would suggest that to set one's soul in silence is to still the noise of our false perceptions that have relegated God to a secondary place in our life and exalted us to primacy. We must still the noise of our false values by which we derange our lives and the world to fulfill our own desires, wants, and purposes. We must still the noisy demands of our behavior patterns that are contrary to being in the image of God.

I would further suggest that to set one's soul in silence is to still those things in our being that distract us from attentiveness to God. We need to still the noise of those dynamics of our lives that disrupt the inner peace of our being. We need to still the noise of those competing and conflicted demands that disturb and unbalance the equilibrium of our spirit.

This cacophony of inner noise is usually associated with where we find the roots of our identity, meaning, value, and purpose. When we find these in anything other than God, we are decentered persons, unstable at the core of our being and consequently pulled in multiple directions by those unstable things in our life upon which we have grounded our identity, meaning, value, and purpose.

In the final analysis, to set one's soul in silence is to detach from all those things in which we have rooted our identity, meaning, value, and purpose apart from God. Since these things have shaped what we call our self, silencing is a losing of that self. This is a tremendous threat. The false self with its false identity, meaning, value, and purpose is the only self we know. If we detach from this, if we set our soul in silence, what will we be? It would seem that we would become persons rooted and grounded in God's love and life, persons who find the true self "hidden with Christ in God" (Col 3:3), persons who come to discover their authentic identity, meaning, value, and purpose in God.

What does it mean to set one's soul in peace? If silencing is detaching from the false self, setting our soul in peace would be the relinquishing of our being to God in loving abandonment like "a weaned child on its mother's breast"; or, in Jesus' words, losing our (false) self for his sake (Matt. 10:39). The power of this image resides in the word *weaned*. The unweaned child is at its mother's breast for what it wants and what it needs—milk! The mother is nothing more than a giver of nourishment. The image of the weaned child at its mother's breast, however, is one of complete and utter abandonment to the mother's love, allowing the mother to be whatever she desires to be with her child, permitting the mother to lavish her love upon her child in whatever manner she deems proper, desiring for the mother to bond her child to her in trusting love.

Listening to the silence, then, is a loving abandonment of ourselves to God; allowing God to be God on God's terms; giving God free rein in our being; permitting God to do in, through, and with us whatever God desires rather than a proactive action on our part to achieve something. This posture of radical abandonment to God is the antithesis of the proud heart that exalts itself as god in its life. This posture of utter forsaking of one's self, losing one's self for God's sake is the antithesis of the haughty eyes that view everything and everyone from a perspective of proud superiority and pervasive self-referencedness.

Listening to the silence, then, is the essence of the life "hidden with Christ in God" (Col. 3:3), not a discrete action performed from time to time. We learn to live life by listening to the silence, and out of that centeredness in God the Word becomes flesh in them.

—Robert Mulholland

# Spirit God Prayer

Spirit God, you know our needs
    our wounds
    our hurts
    our fears
    even before we can form them
        into words of prayer.
You are patient with us.
You are protective of us.
You are present with us
    until such time that we are able
    to ask for what we need.
Thank you, Spirit God,
    for your healing taking place within
    before we are even aware
    of how broken we have become.[8]

—SUSAN GREGG-SCHROEDER

# Ruby Clarity

MY FRIEND REBECCA CALLED one day. To look at us, Rebecca and I have nothing in common. She is ten years younger, a marathon runner, parent, world traveler, and brilliant. What we have in common is our love for each other and the assurance, honed over years of experience, that the other will be there no matter what.

One other thing we have in common is toenail polish. Rebecca paints hers because, apparently, distance runners tend to have bruised and discolored toenails. I polish mine because I like the way it looks.

So Rebecca called that day to say that she had found a new shade of nail polish: "It's called Ruby Clarity. Now, even though nothing else in life is clear, at least our toes will have some Clarity!"

Clarity, that lovely sense of seeing the path of one's life, is a rare and precious gift. Rebecca's discovery of Ruby Clarity came at a particularly difficult time in my life. My husband had just died of cancer, and my grief was laced with questions about the future, what would come next, and how I would learn to bear it. The polish became a touchstone during those dark days when absolutely nothing else felt clear. "What color are your toes?" one of us would ask the other from time to time. I use the polish less and less these days, though it remains on the shelf "just in case."

Nail polish, of course, cannot change the course of one's life. Life is messy and complicated and ambiguous. The shades of gray and nuance that can make life more rich and satisfying can also make it frustrating and scary.

One of the gifts of my life was a week spent in the presence of the great Quaker Douglas Steere who, near the end of his life, had a frail body but strong spirit. Among other things, Douglas taught me the Quaker practice of discernment through a Clearness Committee. A

Quaker seeking clarity on a particular question may call together a group of people to aid in the discernment. The question, with all its implications and possibilities, is put to the group as fully as the convener is able. Out of a time of silence and listening, members of the committee may ask the convener about the decision in question. They may not offer advice or make statements, but the convener may come to "clearness" with the help of those who have listened with her.

Clarity can also come through personal prayer—as gift after I have stilled myself to sit in receptive prayer, waiting openly over days and months. Sometimes clarity comes as surprise, with the realization that the clearness I sought "snuck in" while I wasn't looking and took up quiet residence in my soul.

Clarity often finds me at the Communion rail. On any given Sunday, the chalice bearer is as likely to be a youth as an adult, and those at the rail with me are infants in arms, older adults, folks with mental challenges, others with advanced degrees, and families of varying colors and composition. "Receive your mystery," one of the early church fathers said while standing at the Table.[9] We, the body of Christ, gather at the Table to be fed by that same body to go into the world as that dispersed body, whose other name is Love. When I have eaten Love, when I have consumed and been consumed by Love (the love that casts out fear), clarity is a much more likely.

Wendy Wright related an experience she had while leading her first retreat. She called the story "The Wisdom of the Woman in the Neon Yellow Pantsuit." She distilled that wisdom in this way: "If you can see the big picture, the five-year plan, the long view with no insurmountable hurdles, there's a good chance that it may not be the will of God. However, if all you can see is the next small step and beyond that, nothing, there's a chance that it's the will of God."[10]

Whether we understand the will of God as an immutable master plan composed of great decisions and inconsequential choices or as "the place where your deep gladness and the world's deep hunger meet,"[11] the gift of clarity, of vision, of discernment is one we seek. May you—with Clearness Committee, in contemplative prayer at the Table, or wherever else it may find you—discern the precious gem of Ruby Clarity.

—NANCY BRYAN CROUCH

# MOVING TO
# THE RHYTHM
# OF GRACE

# Riffs of Rising

When, after solstice, finches catch the sun
On wing and sweep, like golden fluting, through
The sky, my eyes are fixed on dirt, not blue
For planting, weeding, reaping must be done.
It's not their flight that penetrates the stun
Of toil but song: gay riffs of rising blue
Grass fiddle phrase, high rondos piercing through
The chink of spade. My waking has begun.

I watch them fall and climb and always, in
The belly of each wave, they sing. You'd think
They'd be more sober. Nesting weighs. The light
Wanes swiftly. Yet they play on currents thin
As breath. Goldfinches push me to the brink
(O teach my heart this buoyancy) of flight.

—LORA MOORE

# Finding a Point of Balance

I'M A BENEDICTINE SISTER of Perpetual Adoration, a Catholic contemplative nun. My community seeks to follow the Gospel of Jesus with the help of a fifteen-hundred-year-old document called the Rule of Benedict. In the Gospels, Jesus commands us to love one another, but he doesn't give details. Who does the dishes; who takes out the trash, does the laundry, attends the meetings; who handles the money; and who makes the decisions? Jesus didn't really answer those questions. Yet, so often these questions and others like them are what get in the way of our loving one another. Benedict of Nursia, around 530 CE, put together a way of living that dealt with many of these questions and has led thousands of people in a balanced way of living the Christian life.

The word *rule* comes from the Latin *regula* and means simply a way to "regulate" our lives. Often we view regulations as negative boundaries to our freedoms, but perhaps we are looking at the term *regulate* from the wrong angle. To regulate an engine means to tune it to run more efficiently. To regulate traffic means to help it flow in a smooth and steady manner. To regulate our hearts is to help them beat in a strong, constant rhythm. Regulation enables us to live well over the long haul. Perhaps some of our immediate impulses are curtailed, but the result is a more balanced existence.

Balance seems to be one of the spiritual disciplines that we often have difficulty practicing in our modern culture. Today, at least in America, we seem to be a people of extremes. We are encouraged to give 110 percent of ourselves to everything we do. We are always plugged in to what's happening around us. However, that doesn't leave much time or space for us to tune in to what is going on inside of us.

Benedict's Rule balanced life upon three legs: prayer, work, and leisure. Benedict believed that these three elements needed to be part of every life every day. Of course, that doesn't mean they were given equal time or equal status. Balance is not always a matter of equal weights poised on a scale. When I was a child, I learned that I could play on seesaws and teeter-totters with children much smaller than me, because balance isn't just a matter of having equal weights; it's a matter of where we place the fulcrum, the balance point.

Benedict's balance point is God's will. Finding God's will requires slowing down enough to be able to get the feel for where we are in balance and out of balance. Work may take more hours than prayer. Yet, if I am not giving enough time for prayer, my work will not flow as smoothly, nor will it accomplish all that it might if God were more involved. If my work and prayer are in balance, but my family and friends are barely there, then I have lost the support of community and my share in it. I need time for prayer, for work, *and* for leisure; and so does everyone else.

Of course, there is more to it than just making time each day for these three things. Within our prayer we need some time for silence and some time for active and communal worship. We need some physical activity and some intellectual activity in our work. We need community and solitude in our leisure. Finding the balance for each individual takes almost as much time and effort as finding the right nutritional balance for each body.

Perhaps it would help to consider some of the signs of being out of balance. I recognize imbalance in myself when I start to feel tired, even after a good night's sleep. When I find myself thinking, *I'm just too tired*, I need to ask, "What am I tired of?" and then give thought to what is out of balance. Have I been working with people too long and need some solitude to rejuvenate myself? Have I been dealing with things and need to spend more time with people? Have I been tackling problems and allowed my responsibilities to overburden and overwhelm me? Maybe I need to spend some time with God and lay some of these burdens at God's feet rather than carrying them on my weak shoulders.

Often we deal with prayer as a task. We turn it into a visit with Santa Claus or a business meeting with the boss. Religious professionals often turn prayer time into ministry planning. But personal prayer time is about loving and being loved by the One who made us and loves us into being every day of our lives. It is not a quantifiable project but a qualitative relationship that requires nurture and attention.

Being "burned out" often signals being unbalanced too long. I think of ball bearings and how they can cause a motor to burn out if they have undergone uneven wear. We need to remember the fuel source of our inner fire while we are still on fire. We need to know what gives us energy and what replenishes our energy after a particularly draining experience. If we are trying to be the source of our own strength, energy, and enthusiasm, the fire will be short-term no matter how bright it seems. If the fuel comes from our relationships with God and others, then we have to return to those relationships to keep the flame burning. While seemingly obvious, many people lose sight of the fire because they focus on the smoke, which often lasts longer than the flames. We can't afford to smolder; we can't afford to let the smoke hide the flame. We need to keep the light shining bright, which requires finding balance.

One way to stay apprised of our balance is to take some planned time apart, get away from the mad tilt-a-whirl of ordinary life that pushes and pulls us from various angles, and see how steady we are when we walk without those gyrating gravitational forces. We can see then if we are walking the straight path or if we wobble.

When I was young in the monastery, we took lessons in wobble-ology, the practice of finding our center by wobbling back and forth between the extremes of life. The center is that place between right and left. It is the space between conservative and liberal, between slow and fast, between taking no responsibility and taking all responsibility. Saint Benedict tells us to keep all things in moderation. Balance is the way of living that exists between my doing everything and God's doing everything.

—SR. DAWN ANNETTE MILLS, OSB

# Drumbeat

A drumbeat,
Simple thread of rhythm,
Woman creates the pulsating, primal pattern.
Inviting one to join,
Then another.
Soon wall and floors
And all held in the dancing cocoon
Rock in the rhythmic groove.
Layer after layer, pulsing, pounding
Filaments of rhythm fill the air,
Stunning tempos of colors,
Diverse sounds and timbres,
Beautiful tapestry of sound and movement.

Dancing begins,
Singing follows:
We are "walking in the light of God."[1]
Drumming and dancing!
Dancing and drumming!

Shakers, sticks, bells, and bodies
Each bearing the sounds of the drums
Thick textures weaving into a crescendo
A full-bodied offering of praise.

Unencumbered procession, now transformed,
Within the sacred silence.
Moving into a different place, a different space,
Into the silence beyond the sound,
Beyond the drumming, beyond the singing,

Toward the light,
To the silence of the heart, the space where images and stories live.

Within that realm, that holy place,
Worshipers find the gifts:
Hope penetrating despair,
Joy rising up out of anguish,
Shalom soothing the troubled spirit.

—JUDY HOLLOWAY

# Morning Rhythm

ON YESTERDAY'S WALK I paused to stand barefoot in the lake. Kaia charged toward the water's edge at me with tongue flying, water flying, spirit flying. She's seven. Her muzzle is prematurely gray; she doesn't run as fast, jump as high, or get into as much mischief as she did a couple of years ago. These moments of play have and shall become increasingly rare; so I delight to encounter them and almost always rouse my stiffening (also aging) self to respond to her invitation.

I dash at her, then stop sharply, and turn abruptly. (*Sharply* and *abruptly* are my terms; my teenaged sons would giggle and refer to my slowing reflexes). I run away; Kaia chases. I turn on her; she crouches then gallops at me. We open-hand/open-paw box. I make ready to grab her sixty-pound black lab/husky self around the middle, but she tears away—as fast as when she chases (but fails to catch) a deer on some of our woodland walks.

I cannot help but laugh. I am out of breath. My hip hurts from trying to avoid falling over a piece of driftwood during the chase. And I am surprised as always after these moments.

This morning routine—bicycling to beach or forest trail, then dismounting to walk the lake's edge or among muttering trees—is intended to keep a minimal level of mobility, fitness, and prayer in my life. It becomes meditation full of quiet wonder at how land and water meet, at how distant islands and mountains sometimes appear to hover over the lake. This meditation—often supported by the regular movement of knee and pedal, the customary click of Kaia's toenails on asphalt, the regular humfph-humfph of Kaia's breath as she runs alongside my bicycle, the constant jingle of her tags—is full of amazement at how day and light and bird song can course into my being and entangle themselves so much with my interior that I must say it is "good and right" to be in this life—even when life is struggle and disappointment, even when life is frightening.

There is clear rhythm and pattern—even ease—around this morning routine: dog jogging quietly, stopping for leisurely exploratory snuffles. Then they are broken—the rhythm, pattern, ease. A high-intensity jolt of abandon, foolishness, risk, and energy springs forth from dog and sometimes, surprisingly, from me! The out-of-breathness and the laughter ripple minor shock waves through who I am. Each cell experiences its own tiny explosive laugh-exhale, forcing out the stale and the toxic. Each cell, at least briefly, is wide awake, exhaling powerfully enough to inhale the world in a more robust way.

And so the rhythm is broken. Or is it? Is there a greater rhythm that requires play, surprise, and the accompanying discomfort and delight to aperiodically mess with our carefully constructed life-giving patterns? Kaia, who has not read the Bible and only occasionally attends lakeside worship, says yes!

—REGINA LAROCHE

# Shadow Dance

I search for wisdom
In the usual places
And finding none,
I look harder
Until I feel a tap
on my shoulder
and turn to face
my shadow.
She reaches out her hand,
inviting me to dance.
Can I really let her lead?
I will need a new step.
I will make mistakes
and not be perfect.
Yet to turn away means
to fail my quest for wisdom
who wears my shadow face.

—DENISE MCGUINESS

# Grounding in Grace

"AS YOU PLACE YOUR HANDS on the mat, root all of your fingers and joints down. Ground yourself in grace. Align your nature with the divine flow of love that is an essential part of you." The yoga teacher's words on grace caused my spirit, which had long been taught about the gift of prevenient grace, to leap to attention.

At the beginning of this yoga practice, surrounded by many fit, young, and lithe bodies, I needed a plethora of grace—to keep from comparing myself as less. In addition, I wasn't sure how difficult this class would become, or when and where my body would betray that I was more of a wannabe yogi than a real practitioner. I was unsure when my body would display the health issues that had brought me to yoga in the first place. With great intensity I pressed my fingers and palms deeply into the mat. *O grace, flow all around me*, I pleaded internally.

A few years before this moment I had experienced terrible pain and neurological damage that resembled a multiple sclerosis (MS) attack. Though I was never diagnosed with MS, I was left with a limp, poor balance, frequent stumbling—and a changed view of what was important in life. Before the attack I had been busily working as a United Methodist pastor in a large suburban parish, spending most of every waking minute trying to nurture a youth ministry and a people while neglecting my body's need for rest and restoration. Though ultimately the etiology of my myelitis remains unknown, my hunch is that stress and overwork may have played a role. My body pointedly taught me that I needed to learn a new way of life, one grounded not in productivity and accomplishment but in the rhythms of grace.

I found switching rhythms to be a challenging move. I would wake in the morning with a beautiful sense of gratitude for each step. By lunch I was rushing around to hospital visits, and in the evening I was literally limping off to my last meeting. Somewhere along the course of the day I forgot to live into the gift of each moment. I stepped out of the flow of grace and into the march of relentless productivity. Learning a new way of life for me would require more than a disease; my healing would require changes in my whole approach to life.

Fast forward a few months and many yoga classes later, and I found myself on my hands and knees listening to a new teacher speak about grace in the beginning of a yoga-teacher training course. By some beautiful providence I had landed in an *anusara*-inspired teacher training; *anusara* means "to flow with grace" and describes a system of yoga that cultivates open hearts and sound biomechanical principles. That style resonated with my own Wesleyan background and desire to heal in body, mind, and spirit.

My spirit began to change as well. I could sit longer in Centering Prayer; I no longer got impatient in lines; and I lived more into a liturgy of the hours. Oh, I still scurried around and reveled too much in busyness—yoga and other spiritual practices didn't transform me into a saint. At least I took deep breaths as I checked off my to-do list!

My mind opened to a much gentler and broader understanding of God. As I studied yoga, I learned about Hinduism, the religion that gave birth to yoga ("union with God") millennia ago. I came to respect deeply the embodied nature of Hindu spirituality and its openness to seeing the sacred in the most mundane aspects of life. The practice of yoga nurtured me into seeing my wounded body as holy— a nurturing that seemed to be lacking in my own Christian tradition, which has had such a deeply ambiguous relationship with the body.

I came to really appreciate Tilden Edwards's words in *Living in the Presence* in which he said, "In the wider ecumenism of the Spirit being opened for us today, we need to humbly accept the learnings of particular Eastern religions in relation to the body. . . . What makes a particular practice Christian is not its source, but its *intent*."[2] My intention in the practice of yoga was to imitate Christ more fully. I learned that my fellow yoga practitioners and I could become beautiful companions on the spiritual journey together, even as I remained committed to my Christian faith. I learned that it wasn't up to me to determine boundaries for the flow of God's grace.

I still limp when tired and am strongly attracted to intense productivity; transformation into a peaceful person seems to be a rather slow process for me. Nonetheless, I am different. When I instruct my students in a beginning *asana* (pose), I say, "Ground yourself in grace." Then I deepen my own breath and smile as one who speaks from the experience of living into a rhythm of grace.

—MELANIE DOBSON HUGHES

# I Am a Song Sung Forth by God

The song begins.
I am hummed by God.

Intricately written, precisely put together in measure and notes, in
rhythm and rhymes, I am formed.

On sheets of lined paper, the Grand Musician creates.
Am I a waltz, a concerto, a cantata, a hymn?
Will I be played out in great philharmonic halls or whistled through
the fields of an Ohio farm?

Who will conduct me? Could it be that I will solo?

Deep within the very soul of me, I am played by unseen hands;
I am the harmony in a love song only God knows.

Singing of me with the abandonment of self, I play out the mystical
music of life with Christ.

—Cathie McFadden

# Grace of Spiritual Gardening

In the den of a friend's home hangs a photograph of his grandfather (circa 1920)—restored, enlarged, and tinted with pastels. The young man, a truck gardener wearing bib top and a cap, stands with pride, leaning on the truck, canvas sides rolled up, left hand on hip, the other on the right front post of the truck box. Displayed in the truck bed and ready for delivery to the grocer are eight lugs of fresh-picked strawberries.

A generation later this gardener, now a grandfather, profoundly shaped my friend's life. Grandfather would take grandson along as he worked the garden, now known as Sunkist Gardens. Each time he would explain what he was doing and why he did what he did. He loved gardening and shared that love. He was proud of the vegetable plants he grew for sale, proud of the asparagus, the tomatoes, bell peppers, and muskmelons. A specialty was strawberries; he had developed a variety of his own from the old Dunlop stock.

Many years have passed since those days. Recently, however, when a candidate for elder's ordination invited this friend to be a sponsoring elder, she described him as one who was "a gardener of her spirit." He liked that. His story and affirmation started my thinking again about gardening and its place in the life of faith.

The biblical narrative begins with a story set in a garden—the garden of Eden. The story is rich with imagery of God's expectation that humans will care for the garden—God's garden. Some think that this garden was a special piece of ground on the earth, but I believe that the garden was the earth itself and that the eventual exclusion from the garden was not so much relocation as a radical reworking of the relationship among humans, the earth, and God. We humans failed to tend the garden as we were asked.

Therefore, the garden degenerated from a place where God, humans, and all creation dwelt together into a place where humans hid from God and thought they could take matters into their own hands. Forbidden fruit? Who says so? Why not eat it too? We might become as smart as God. We might become God's equals. We might wrest control from the Creator and take over ourselves. Thus the garden's idyllic nature changed even before the expulsion of Adam and Eve. They had already expelled themselves from the life they once had led.

Another major Bible story takes place in a garden: the garden of Gethsemane and the first encounter with the resurrected Christ. Mary Magdalene has come to the empty tomb and sees someone in the garden. I'm particularly fond of the following line in John's Gospel: "Supposing him to be the gardener," she quizzes him about Jesus (John 20:15). Gardener he is but not the gardener she had thought. She has encountered the risen Christ.

Gardeners. That's what God calls us to be. As people of faith, our gardening takes many forms. The most basic of these is the most literal: we are called to tend the earth—God's garden. The earth is not our possession but God's. We are the ones to whom God has entrusted the care of earthly creation. Ecological responsibilities rest on our shoulders. If God's garden—the earth—continues to deteriorate, it is because those to whom God has entrusted it are failing in its care. If global warming continues as human pollution destroys the ozone layer, the onus is ours. Gardening the earth is our God-given responsibility as human beings, one we can deny only at our own peril.

Another type of gardening to which those in leadership are particularly, though not exclusively, called is the gardening of the spirits of other human beings. How are spirits fed and watered and encouraged to grow? Are weeds pulled? Is every human being encouraged and aided to become the wonderful being that God created him or her to be? This is our basic gardening responsibility.

Some time ago I felt I had lost my vital energy for ministry. I could not continue being a spiritual gardener without a spiritual turning point. I felt and saw the dryness in my own garden and began an urgent search for an alternate way. A rich opportunity presented itself, and I spent time in solitude and in community four weeks a year for two years, going deeper on my spiritual journey. I spent my time exploring the presence of God. The retreat faculty became spiritual mentors and guides, skilled and loving gardeners, who led me to taste of God's grace. That rhythm, community, teaching, silence, and worship have shaped and guided my life ever since that experience.

During one of those weeks away, I felt God was pursuing me. Forgotten longings stirred in my heart, and the refrain of a familiar hymn echoed in the inmost chambers of my soul, reminding me of God's everlasting love and claim on my life.

That moment was filled with grace, affirming my soul and enabling me to rejoice in God's presence. Living in God's presence intoxicates us with a passion to love God and God's world. When we live in the presence of God, we recognize ourselves as both garden and gardener, in need of care and created for caring.

—HEE-SOO JUNG

# Transcendent Moments on Our Journey

— ⌁ —

THE RHYTHM OF A DISTANT DRUM woke us on our first morning in Chartres, France. From our hotel breakfast table we glimpsed a small parade, two blocks over, with a marching band and a following of townsfolk. The hotelier explained the group had gathered earlier in the cemetery at the edge of town to honor the war dead. This was Armistice Day. Now they were making pilgrimage to the cathedral for a memorial service.

My wife and I were making pilgrimage too. The opportunity of a long-hoped-for visit to Chartres Cathedral had come about on short notice. Disappointingly, our Friday arrival had been two weeks too late to walk the labyrinth of Chartres. Saturday's affordable guided tour was unavailable because of a special service. Feeling a day late and a Euro short, we succumbed to jet lag and took a late breakfast. The insistent drumbeat captivated our attention. Our hospitable hotelier encouraged us to join the procession.

We jogged through flower-lined streets to catch up with this band of people on the move. We made our way toward the spires of Our Lady of Chartres visible on the hill. Breathlessly and with hearts pounding, we rounded a corner, and her dominating façade came into full view. Her huge central doors were open wide, welcoming all. The procession had already arrived. The band positioned itself outside, continuing to play as the last of us entered. The massive doors closed behind us, silencing the band, and cuing magnificent organ voluntaries to fill the sanctuary.

Just yesterday we'd been allowed to enter Chartres Cathedral only through a small side door to discover her dank, echoing cavernous vaults dimly lit by burning prayer candles. We had lit a candle for Charlie, a covenant companion now dying, who'd once preached on

God being as close as (blow on your hand) a breath away. Yesterday, muted shades of centuries-old rock carvings bore witness to prayers murmured in sacred chancel space normally reserved for clergy on high holy days. Today, we crossed her threshold leaving a world of cold, gray rain and entered the shining radiance of a sanctuary whose light magnified the world's finest collection of Gothic stained glass.

Down the wide center aisle, our footsteps crossed the labyrinth's central rose. Final strains of the voluntary swept over us as we sat in wooden chairs arrayed across the worn stone floor near beautiful, aging French women wearing coats, mufflers, and gloves. Golden chrysanthemums and white and yellow daisies hugged the base of the modest table that seemed dwarfed in the large space. On it was the host—the bread for Holy Communion. The parish priest, dressed in full vestments, began with prayer and introduced the red-capped cardinal who spoke that day.

We do not speak French but could discern part of the message. John 15 was read. We made out the phrases: "No one has greater love than this, to lay down one's life for one's friends. . . . You did not choose me but I chose you. . . . Go and bear fruit, fruit that will last . . . so that you may love one another" (vv. 13, 16, 17). In his homily, the cardinal used words like *egalitaire, libertad, brothers, Resistance, martyrs, saints, freedom, love*. From his voice inflection, we understood questions such as these: What brings us here—a national holiday? remembrance of the sacrifices of fallen heroes, martyrs of the Resistance? patriotism? gratitude for liberties? Or is it, he asked, the One in whom all find freedom, peace, and life abundant—the living Christ?

Caught up in the universality of the service, we still felt a bit like onlookers until a solemn yet familiarly cadenced recitation began. Everyone participated. By the third phrase we recognized words of the Lord's Prayer and joined using English. The cardinal and the priest took Communion on behalf of all gathered, then led the community in an ancient profession of faith, the Apostles' Creed. Remarkably, our English kept up with French phrasings. We were united in the rhythm of the liturgy. It could have been any commemorative service of worship; the liturgy held us. There could have been any homilist; the liturgy encompassed everyone. Had it been a tiny chapel in a remote setting, the rhythm of the liturgy would still have been sustained.

Through the rhythm of the mass and the mystery of the Eucharist, the fire of the Holy Spirit rained down. This moment of our Chartres pilgrimage became a transcendent one in our spiritual journey. Belief in the holy catholic church and the communion of saints took on new meaning in a sea of grace-filled community gathered in Christ.

The special service seemed to end as quickly as it had begun. The priest blessed us with a good word. When the recessional began, we noticed an old man wearing a foreign legion hat and carrying a flag containing a great number of streaming campaign ribbons. Although his body was hunched over and he limped, there was a humble dignity about him. A light that was not his own seemed to shine from his eyes. Tears streamed from ours as we filed down the aisle, back across the labyrinth rose. A closing organ voluntary crowned the glory of those final moments inside the cathedral.

The recessional birthed us into a glistening morning transformed by crisp air and warm sunshine. As the great doors flung wide, the little band struck up again; and we joined the march back into the world.

Both our experiences of Chartres that week are indicative of our spiritual journeys: sacred moments in the darkness and transcendent moments that catch us by surprise. We are grateful to God who can break through darkness or disappointment anytime, anywhere and help us remember God's glory and our union with humankind. Our hearts are still afire with God's unexpected grace in holy mystery, breathtaking beauty, rhythm of the liturgy, renewed connection, shared gratitude, and the utter fullness of Christ.

—LINDA AND BILLY KEEN

# LIVING COMMUNITY/ LIVING FLAMES

# A Divine Invitation

My heart
Like yours
Aches under the weight
Of humanity's pain.

Distractions offer soothing but superficial relief
Food. Television. The Mall.

But from the heart's pure center
A divine invitation echoes
Love God; love your neighbor as yourself.
Bring your gaze to the difficult,
The heartbreaking thing,
The overwhelming situation,
The tragic circumstance,
That hopeless place.
Turn your attention, your gaze, yourself,
To the poor
And be uncomfortable.

How easily we forget, lose sight of the vastness of God's love
The depth of mercy poured out upon us.
To love God is to allow God
To give us God's heart
To fill us with compassion
And steadfast serenity
That we might never weary of loving our neighbors,
Becoming for them God's vessel of grace and hope and healing
In the Golgothas of our world.

Could it be that my aching for the anguish of the world
Is the feeling of my heart being enlarged?
Could it be that my willingness to ache for my suffering neighbor
Is my purest assent to God's perfect intent?

—ROBERT CARR

# Body of Christ

He has told you, O mortal, what is good;
and what does the LORD require of you
but to do justice, and to love kindness
and to walk humbly with your God?
—Micah 6:8

ON APRIL 30, 2006, an estimated 3,000 to 5,000 people spanned the Golden Gate Bridge in San Francisco and joined hands in silent vigil to bring attention to the dire situation in Darfur, a region within the African country of Sudan. An estimated 15,000 attended the afternoon rally on Crissy Field. In Washington DC that same day, 760,000 postcards were delivered to the White House with an estimated crowd of 75,000 attending a rally on the National Mall. Eight members of the Save Darfur Coalition had met with President Bush the previous Friday.

As my high school son, Chris, and I joined hands and raised our arms in silent vigil with the thousands of others on the Golden Gate Bridge that morning, the full impact of what we were representing and standing for hit me. I wept with a suffering heart at my realization that I was a voice for victims in Darfur who desperately needed the world to know their story and not be forgotten. As the cars whizzed by, many honking in support, and as people not part of the vigil walked by, it created a visual analogy of how easy it is for us to go on in our day-to-day lives and not realize or think about the experience of others who are not part of our immediate sphere of existence.

Only a few weeks earlier I was among those oblivious to Darfur until I casually perused the ushers' desk and discovered a flyer about obtaining a free DVD on Darfur to share with the congregation. The information on the flyer compelled me to go to a meeting at the nearby Presbyterian church that was sponsoring a viewing and distribution of the DVD and to hear what other groups and churches were already doing. Afterward, I scheduled a Sunday at our Christian Formation hour to show the DVD and invited a speaker from a local Save Darfur chapter not only to tell more about the situation but also to present options for action. This led to my standing on the Golden Gate Bridge on a Sunday morning understanding and experiencing fully what the body of Christ looks and feels like and what it is that Christ is calling us to do—to care for and tend to his flock, even those we don't know.

I also realized how a church can be the body of Christ through postcards. Members and friends of Walnut Creek United Methodist Church, my home church, added nearly 100 voices of advocacy through postcards.

These rallies, vigils, and postcards did not go unnoticed. The following Monday the White House sent Deputy Secretary of State Robert Zoellick to Nigeria to help salvage peace negotiations. On Friday, May 5, the government of Sudan and the largest of the rebel groups in Darfur agreed to a peace plan that paved the way for United Nations peacekeeping troops to enter. Before this, the Sudanese government had steadfastly refused to receive any UN forces.

This fragile peace plan did not eliminate the threat of genocide. The hard work goes on in keeping the world's awareness of the situation maintained through that small radar screen of the news media.

If I had not been swimming in rich spiritual waters, would I have noticed that flyer? I don't know. What I do know is that there is no such thing as coincidence, only providence, and that being intentional in deepening my awareness of God's presence in my life is one of the most important things I can do. My life and that of others depends on it. As a disciple of Christ, I can do no less.

—JAN SECHRIST

# Community and Communion in Paysandú

THANK GOD FOR THE LOAF and cup because not only did we get off to a less-than-auspicious start but later the whole endeavor seemed headed for absolute disaster. I was a United Methodist missionary working as the pastor of the Methodist congregation in Paysandú, Uruguay. We were receiving a work team from the United States to help us repair the church's roof. For the fifteen who came from the States, Latin America was a new experience. Except for me, the congregation had had little interaction with Americans.

In Uruguay any social occasion (even a business meeting) does not get underway until everyone has personally greeted everyone else. It is considered rude in the extreme to enter into people's social space and not acknowledge them, so a delegation from the congregation had gone with me to meet the bus on which the Americans were coming, with plans to welcome each and every member of the work team.

However, the Americans, like most task-oriented work teams, were anxious to get the show on the road. They were so focused on retrieving their luggage, getting to the church, and checking out the roof that they apparently did not see the Uruguayan offers of handshakes. This seeming rebuff initially baffled and then angered the church delegation—not a good way to start. And it would get worse.

The members of the church in Paysandú were blue-collar folk—factory workers and strong union members. They were also left-leaning in their politics. The Americans who had come to work on the roof were pretty much the polar opposite.

In conversations at night, after the day's work on the roof, the Uruguayans vigorously sought to engage the Americans in conversation and even debate, challenging and probing to see the extent of the Americans' knowledge of and agreement with the US government's complicity in helping to bring Uruguay's human-rights-violating military dictatorship to power (1973–85). With the language barrier, I found myself translating back and forth late into the night.

The Americans felt uncomfortable with the conversation; the Uruguayans continued to push. Finally, some of the work team expressed considerable displeasure at the suggestion that they or their country were somehow responsible for the mess in Uruguay. Tempers flared; recriminations were exchanged. The situation became quite strained.

Although the group managed to get work done on the roof, as we gathered for the final meal together, the Americans sat on one side of the table and the Uruguayans on the other. It looked like the stand-off it had become. So at meal's end, I asked the group to stand, then sit back down alternating American and Uruguayan around the table. I then told them that we were going to close our time together by celebrating Holy Communion—but with a twist. I was not going to serve them but, rather, they were going to serve each other. After the words of institution in both Spanish and English, each person was to pass the bread to his or her left and then be served by the person to whom it had just been passed. The same was true with the cup; American serving Uruguayan, Uruguayan serving American, and so on. Each was to say in his or her own language, "The body of Christ broken for you. The blood of Christ shed for you."

Unlike the day of Pentecost, when each heard God's word in his or her own language (Acts 2:8), the power of that Communion moment in Paysandú was that each one heard in the *other person's* language, as each one served the other and was in turn served by the other.

As the loaf and cup made their way around that table, something broke, fell away, or came upon us. By the time the elements came full circle, there was a very different energy in the room than when we had begun.

Although liturgically out of sequence, when all had served and been served, I asked the group to stand and pass the peace. At that point, eye contact was made; names were spoken, even if mispronounced; handshakes were offered (and this time received); and people fell into each other's arms, some weeping, others laughing. As we made our way to the bus station to bid the work team good-bye, people exchanged names and addresses, promising to write.

The celebration of Communion that day did not erase the cultural or language differences between the two groups. It did not undo history or complicity in that history. It did not even say that, deep down, we are all the same.

The Communion in Paysandú reminded us that, despite all of the things that separate us (some of them quite serious, indeed), we are vitally connected to one another nonetheless as sisters and brothers in Christ and are called to live with each other accordingly. That Communion affirmed that all of us are part of the community of the many/*muchos* for whom Christ's blood of the New Covenant was poured out. Thank God, for the loaf and cup.

—RANDALL R. HANSEN

# Praying for Community

WE GATHER, O GOD, with a new awareness of community. Our reunion with familiar companions of the journey and our notice of strangers in our midst enliven us to the wonder of the other. Tutor our spirits to embrace the newness of community and to embrace your newness with us.

Thank you, O God, for the gift of relationship. Even though our very survival and nurture depend on this gift, we often imagine that we can prevail alone. Our illusion of independence has sometimes come from traumas and betrayals in community. We want to distance ourselves from any possibility of repeating such pain. Some of us have suffered the anguish of being strangers in our own homeland. And some of us have suffered indifference to our cries, tears, and infirmities. We have so many reasons to doubt that your gift to us is for us. Heal our wounds, we pray. Stop our flinching and fleeing when possibilities for intimacy arise. Tutor our spirits to embrace our need for your gift of community.

We confess that times arise when we not only reject your gift of community; we also reject you. Our disappointments with others easily become our disappointment with you. Still, we strongly feel the call to relationships . . . and to you. O God, continue to gather with us even though we murmur our complaints and fail to keep covenant with you. Tutor our spirits to savor and rejoice in community.

Help us to care for your gift: to invest our time and energy in institutions, systems, protests, and service that honor your movement of love in all creation. We often perceive ourselves as too impotent to end the violence against your creation—its people, creatures small and large, land, air, and water. Our fears drive us to demand quick solutions regardless of the devastation we cause for generations to come.

We are embarrassed to admit that we trust our old oppressive remedies more than we trust who you call us to be. Tutor our spirits to be good stewards and all that sustains community.

In the midst of our awareness, gratitude, confession, and plea for help, we long for a time and place of resting in and with you. And perhaps you long to rest with us. Could it be that your gift of community is not only a place where you sustain us to labor, serve, and play but also a place where you await us to rest? Our hearts take delight in the possibility, and they come to a restful assurance as you tutor our spirits to pray . . . to pray. Amen.

—Luther E. Smith Jr.

# Praying Together

IT IS WINTER in Wisconsin. The pale light of early morning gradually spreads itself out over the chapel pews where we are quietly gathered, most of us fresh from sleep. The silence is palpable: deep, rich, and full.

"Psalm 63," the prayer leader gently prompts, and we turn the pages of our worshipbooks to find the familiar words laid out before us. We open our lips and our breaths are swept up together into one common melody:

"In the morning I will sing glad songs of praise to you."

What are we doing when we begin the day this way? When we also end the day together with the ancient and familiar words: "Lord, you let your servant go in peace . . . "? How is it that we are thus being shaped by this shared prayer into the persons God created us to be?

What we are doing is not an innovation. It was what the earliest Christians did before there were church buildings or even a common day off to observe Sunday, the Lord's Day. They gathered in the morning and the evening to pray. In so doing they made, and we make, God and the things of God the first and last thoughts of the day. In a sense we sanctify time, make it holy. We honor the human rhythms of waking and sleeping and the earth's rhythms of sunrise and sunset. We surround our day with the parentheses of prayer, setting it apart for God.

The early Christians did this in common, using shared and ancient words. There is a particular grace to sharing a common prayer. Whenever or wherever we pray, we are not alone. Prayer allows us access to the eternity of God's own time. In that time we are present not only to the divine but to each other. We are present to all those who pray, all over the earth, in diverse gestures and languages. We are also present to those who have prayed and who will pray: in the early church, in the intervening centuries, and in the centuries to come.

When we enter into prayer using shared and ancient words, we are using many of the same words that those early Christians did. We are ushered into a vast, infinitely rich reservoir of longing and hoping that is larger than ourselves. For millennia certain psalms and canticles have been associated with specific times of prayer. Psalm 63 and the Canticle of Zachary (Luke 1:68-79, which prophesies the coming of the light to illuminate the darkness) have long been associated with morning prayer. Evening prayer is traditionally observed with the Magnificat, the Canticle of Mary (Luke 1:46-55) and with Psalm 141, the "incense psalm" ("My prayers rise like incense, my hands like the evening offering," JB). Similarly, the day ends with night prayer, which includes the Canticle of Simeon (Luke 2:29-32) with its sentiments of peaceful reception: "Now I can go in peace, my eyes have seen the salvation meant for the nations."

We are shaped by the words we pray. When we pray the Lord's Prayer deeply, our lips and hearts give articulation to the core of our faith. So it is with the psalms and canticles that form the backbone of the daily liturgies. We are expanded by the praise ("My soul proclaims the greatness of the Lord"), summoned by the hope ("Blessed be the God of Israel who comes to set us free"), met in our lament ("Out of the depths I cry to you"), and consoled by the words into which we enter ("In the shadow of your wings, I sing for joy. I cling to you, your hand keeps me safe").

When we sing we heighten our praying. We gather up breath and body; we give form and flight to our hearts' keenest longings. Our whole selves engage in what we pray. "My whole being desires you like a dry, worn, waterless land," we sing, and the notes take the shape of our desire; they trace our thirst and ache with our longing for God.

All this happens when we sing these daily liturgies alone. But when we pray together, we come to know that we are small streams that run into wider, deeper channels that in turn flow into the vast ocean of prayer. We are made aware of the depth of our connection with one another. We become mindful of our common hope, our shared longing. We are also made conscious that we live that common hope in diverse and individual ways. Our commonality is not a rigid uniformity but a convergence at the level of our common humanity and our communion in Christ.

When our prayer is guided by the simple form of the liturgies of daily prayer (invocation, psalmody, scripture, canticle, the Lord's Prayer, benediction), we are praying with the ecumenical Christian community. For these daily liturgies, in simplified or more elaborated form, are practiced by Methodists, Lutherans, Presbyterians, Anglicans (Episcopalians), Roman Catholics, Eastern Orthodox, and other Christians.

"Come let us sing to the LORD," the psalmist exhorts us. Yes, let us pray this way together and be formed into the people God intends us to be.[1]

—WENDY WRIGHT

# Sojourners in Faith

Come along with me
    as a sojourner in faith.
Bring along
    a sense of expectancy
    a vision of high hopes
    a glimpse of future possibility
    a vivid imagination
For God's creation is not done.
We are called to pioneer forth
    toward a future yet unnamed.
As we venture forward,
    we leave behind our desires for
    a no-risk life
    worldly accumulations
    certainty of answers.
Let us travel light
    in the spirit of faith and expectation
    toward the God of our hopes and dreams.

Let us be a witness
    to God's future breaking in.
Come along with me
    as a sojourner in faith
    secure in the knowledge
    that we never travel alone.[2]

—SUSAN GREGG-SCHROEDER

# More Than Fast Food

Thomas Merton put forward a test for the church and its ministry that I would like to reissue for today: "What do we have to offer the world that the world doesn't already have more of than it needs?"[3] The word is clear. John 6:26-38 may be summarized with these words from the "Hinson" translation: "Human beings shall not live by bread alone, that is, not their kind of bread. Oh, yes, bread they need, but manna is not enough. They need the living Bread, which comes down from heaven, the Bread that lasts forever. They need God!"

The world seems bent on creating more manna. We need not dwell long on it, but I mention below some of the "mannas" that the world already is sated with and gorged on.

- ITEM ONE. *Self-indulgence as a right.* Some years ago Charles Reich warned in *The Greening of America* about "Consciousness III," the heightening of what some would call "selfish privatism" to the point that society, community, cannot exist. Self-indulgence leaves its marks on every essential facet of our lives—food, sex, work, play, transportation, spirituality.[4]

- ITEM TWO. *Belief that "a little more" will assure happiness.* It's an attitude that I trace back to people of my generation, those who grew up during the Great Depression and the Second World War. We often didn't have enough.

  When the economy recovered and the war ended, it let loose all of our demons of desire. We could have anything we wanted. We now find ourselves whirled around in a system sustained by a creed that a little more will bring the ultimate happiness.

- ITEM THREE. *A conviction that violence and terror will solve the world's problems.* In this post 9/11 world, who is not conscious that people such as Osama bin Laden and nations such as Iraq and Israel, and, yes, the United States, have fallen prey to the false notion that the sword will solve earth's inequities and injustices?

Bloated, teased, and tempted by our culture's distractions, we may find it hard to see that our deepest need remains unmet. This inner craving is the homing instinct Augustine fingered at the beginning of his *Confessions*: "You arouse [us] to take joy in praising you, for you have made us for yourself, and our heart is restless until it rests in you."[5]

In our Gospel lesson Jesus reminds us, first and foremost, that though we need bread that satisfies our daily needs, we need even more the Bread that alone will satisfy the purpose for which God has made us. We need the living God, the One who has tabernacled among us and indeed goes on dwelling among us forever.

You will recognize that we are dealing with one of the "I AM" sayings in the Gospel of John when we hear Jesus say, "I am the bread of life." The Gospel writer wants us to recognize his theology of the Lord's Supper or the Eucharist: every time we observe Eucharist, we call to the world's attention that though the world needs perishable bread, it needs even more the imperishable Bread.

Too many ministers and churches offer the world what it already has more of than it needs. Our culture beats, hammers, stuffs, and engraves us until we fit securely into its own mold. By its very nature the free-enterprise, democratic society we have created lives by marketing, including the marketing of religion. Some people seem to make a success of the marketing of religion. But does the cost for those who buy into what is sold glut them on what they already have more of than they need to the point that it dampens the meaning of their lives?

So we find ourselves sounding like the disciples. "What *sign* will you do so we may see and believe you?" (AP).

To every Christian community the living Christ, the I AM, comes with this simple but stunning message: "*I* am the bread of life. Whoever comes to me will never be hungry, and whoever believes in me will never be thirsty" (John 6:35, emphasis added). Of us the Christ asks, "Do you come and do you believe enough to know that this Bread is what the world needs above and beyond what it already has more of than it needs? Will your community, seeking to live by the spirit of God, do the things that awaken the world's people to the 'Bread come down from heaven,' which, if they partake, never perishes?"

I believe the central purpose of the church and its ministry today may be summarized as *awakening people everywhere, in all cultures and in all religions and in all circumstances, to the Bread that never perishes.* Every Eucharist challenges us, "Will you live by fast food alone? Will you eat only manna that perishes? Or will you let your participation in this sacrament open your inner eyes to God with us?"

To assist with this awakening, to be midwives of grace, we need not only to proclaim but also to *be* bits of this Bread in our relationship to others. We are to be icons of the Icon of the invisible God. To suggest that we mortals can do this is daunting and intimidating and rightly so. *Cura animae,* "care of the soul," is daunting; let's admit it. No human being should come to the ministry of spiritual direction thinking, *I can do it.* Better we should come quaking in our boots, knowing that we take on a task far beyond our natural powers or abilities or skills. Here then is the paradox of spiritual formation: by *nature* nobody's able; by *grace* anybody's able. It's a matter of the Living Word who tabernacled among us coming to tabernacle in us and to touch the lives of others through us. As I would envision our situation, then, we who would serve as instruments of grace should spend a lot of time letting grace irradiate us like the sun's rays constantly irradiate our earth.

And with George Herbert we would do well to pray,

> Teach me, my God and King,
> In all things thee to see,
> And what I do in anything,
> To do it as for thee.[6]

—E. GLENN HINSON

# Wrestling in Community

WE WERE ASSIGNED! That's the first thing I found out about our so-called covenant group. Everything inside of me balked at the very thought of being placed together with a small group of people without any choice—and for two years at that! To begin with, this entire spiritual-formation endeavor was alien territory for me. Many people in the retreat community participated in denominations and theologies that were not my typical evangelical context. Questions about other members of the group plagued me, and from the very first day I felt like I was losing control. I had no means of creating my ideal group and scripting the outcome.

The first group meeting confirmed my worst fears. I did not connect with anybody except a fellow Baptist who was surely not as true-blooded a Baptist as I deemed myself.

*Could I have made a huge mistake by committing myself to this community?* This became my nagging thought throughout the first week of my stay at the retreat center. I came away from that first week feeling quite unsure whether to continue, but somehow I did. Each encounter with this community always spelled out a challenge for me. I disagreed with each of the members on numerous issues and countless occasions. The struggle mounted each meeting. Many times I wished I was in another place or with another group of people.

But I continued. The process, while rough and tough, was worth every whit of conversation, striving for understanding, getting acquainted, and sharing our hearts and lives. For me, community took on a whole different meaning as a result of this experience that I had almost abandoned.

Something happened! I don't recall when and how—it just happened. Covenant group members were the same. The format and topics of our time together never changed dramatically. But beyond any doubt, I was not the same. God changed me in ways that took me totally by surprise. *I* began seeing people and situations in a different manner. I loosened up. Differences between people that I once thought were glaring slowly faded into the distance. The issues that I regarded as significant barriers no longer mattered. I even saw past our personality quirks. Even more surprisingly, I started feeling a connection to each one of them.

So what really happened? "Love took my hand." That's a phrase from one of George Herbert's famous poems that I came upon years ago. For some reason, this registered in my consciousness and helped explain what happened to me. From the community that I thought I would dread forever, I received love as I had not previously experienced. Love took my hand—the same hand that could have remained closed because of my smugness; the hand that could have refused to reach out to those who were unlike me; the hand that could have continued to use its fingers to point judgmentally at others' faults.

Often I came to the group insecure, confused, panicked, stressed-out, harassed, wallowing in self-pity—and unconditional love reached out to me through this community. I felt understood, accepted, and embraced like I have never felt in any other community. All of my prejudices started melting down because of the members' genuine and generous love. My judgmental spirit evaporated into thin air. My intolerance and rigidity subsided, and I felt thoroughly humbled by it all.

It became crystal clear to me: love is indeed the oil that lubricates community—not our sense of rightness, not our purity of doctrine, not our human rituals, and certainly not our well-structured systems and programs. It is love in action that can change lives. Sticking it out with my covenant community allowed love to change my life, my perspectives, my convictions, my entire concept of community radically.

In hindsight, only God could have assigned us together. For this, I am forever grateful!

—WIL HERNANDEZ

# A Blessing Liturgy for Caregivers

Leader: May we each be in prayer as these friends before us offer their hearts for service.

Community: **Blessed are the poor in spirit—the kingdom of heaven is theirs.**

Leader: As you go in humility, imagine offering yourself as you are, not with the idea of solving the problems of the one you visit but simply being present with them in their distress. You will be given God's healing nearness. In fact, in your being there, you and the one for whom you care will participate in the kingdom of heaven and a living sense of the communion of love.

Community: **Blessed are those who mourn—they will be consoled.**

Leader: As you offer your presence to someone in grief, he or she will receive God's comfort through you. Comfort may not seem readily apparent, but the one you visit will feel remembered and loved and will know that their loss matters to you and to God. In turn, you will feel the nearness of God for any grief that may linger in your own heart.

Community: **Blessed are the gentle—they will inherit the land.**

Leader: As you go in gentleness, you carry the gift of God in you. Gentleness is not a lack of confidence but rather a caring attitude that offers a safe space and a listening heart. As you sit in that space with another and listen with love, you will be given the words to say if words are needed. You will be given patience to offer silence if silence is needed. Trust Jesus to love through you.

**Community:** **Blessed are those who hunger and thirst for justice—they will have their fill.**

**Leader:** As you care for the needs of others—a gift of kindness that everyone in the world rightly deserves—you will bring the bread of love and the cup of compassion. This love, this compassion will ease their hunger and thirst for kindness and care in a time of need.

**Community:** **Blessed are those who show mercy to others—they will be shown mercy.**

**Leader:** As you give your time, compassion, and words of comfort to others, what you give will be multiplied back to you. The math in God's kingdom indicates that giving is not subtraction but multiplication. Good stewardship requires that you care for your own energies (with rest, healthy eating, prayer, and play). But joy also comes in knowing that God sees your gift of mercy and that you are keeping the flow of love going in God's kingdom.

**Community:** **Blessed are those whose hearts are clean—they will see God.**

**Leader:** As you offer care to another, don't try to be more than you are. Be yourself. Go in the simplicity of love, which does not require that you have just the right word or nugget of wisdom to offer. If you stumble, talk too much, or forget to ask about something important, do not despair! Just offer your heart before God—asking for mercy, wisdom, and strength; and keep going. God will be there. God will shine through you to the other.

**Community:** **Blessed are those who work for peace—they will be called children of God.**

**Leader:** Offering care to another is a work *of* peace, a work *for* peace. A certain kind of peace comes to the other simply in being remembered, in feeling connected to the larger Christian community. Indeed, you offer healing and grace-bearing peace.

—STEPHANIE FORD

*Leaders may lay hands on caregivers and anoint their heads with oil saying,* "(Name of person), you are anointed as grace bearer in the name of the Prince of Peace."

PRAYER:

God of all compassion, anoint these sisters and brothers with your gift of tender care. Kindle their hearts with a Christlike love. Give them the ability to see the needs of the world and the strength and humility to touch those needs with your grace. Help them to bring their true self, their best self, made in your image, to each relationship. Bless them to be blessings for others. And in all these compassionate encounters, may your name be glorified through Christ, who brings healing and peace. Amen.

—CYNTHIA LANGSTON KIRK

# Encountering Resurrection

EASTER, LIKE THE MYSTERY of Christ's resurrection, always lies in wait for us, even when we embrace its joy. Resurrection, for this age, seems unreal. It is death that appears real. Death and suffering. Pain and strife. What the news media report and show over and over again. But is it the images that seem real or the death? We are fascinated by and drawn to the images of death and war and suffering, bombs and gunfire, fascinated with terror and grief. This is why resurrection seems so difficult—this coming back from, this overcoming of death.

In Acts 5 Peter's claim that God raised Jesus from the dead is met with incredulity and even rage. Had it not been for the wise Pharisee named Gamaliel, Peter and the others would have been killed.

The story of Thomas confronts us with this difficulty about resurrection. He wasn't with the others on that first Easter evening, hiding behind closed doors, when Jesus appeared speaking shalom and showing them his wounded hands and side. We shouldn't be too hard on Thomas. His doubts are what the actuality of the world teaches us. For we, like Thomas, live here—caught between the actuality of the world as it is and the world as it ought to be. Between the world presented to our senses and the world as we hope it might be; between the broken world where death seems to have the last word and a dream of a redeemed, healed, joy-giving, just world: this is where we live.

Poet and hymn text writer Thomas Troeger has captured this well in his hymn "These Things Did Thomas Count as Real," as he speaks of "the warmth of blood, the chill of steel."[7] For Thomas the idea of someone raised from the dead simply did not make sense. Yet Jesus does not despise Thomas's uncertainty, does he? Rather Jesus offers Thomas the opportunity to see and touch that he might be convinced. Then Thomas recognizes, "My Lord and my God!" (John 20:28).

The shock is this: Thomas wished to see, to touch, to hear the real Jesus—not simply the unbelievable story that Jesus was raised from the dead. In Thomas's touching and seeing, what is real and what is unreal is forever reversed! Here the whole of John's Gospel stands unveiled: "'Blessed are those who have not seen and yet have come to believe'" (20:29). The witness of John and the testimony of the followers: Mary and the women, Peter (who in John 21 is asked those embarrassing questions after breakfast!), and Thomas in need of tangibility . . . these too, along with the others, bear witness that this resurrection is no idle tale.

This reminds me of an image from Matthew Bridges's hymn "Crown Him with Many Crowns," in which Bridges sings of Christ's wounds, even after the Resurrection and the Ascension: "those wounds, yet visible above."[8] So the Resurrection also means that Jesus Christ still carries the signs of his suffering for us. The risen Christ is the wounded healer. God loves the world so much that he sent his only Son to share our life and our own brokenness. This is the stunning rhythm of God with us. How shall we love in return?

One of my favorite passages of Saint Augustine's is found in Book X of his *Confessions*. He prays this question to God: "What am I loving when I love you?" He answers himself in this fashion:

> Not beauty of body nor transient grace, not this fair light, . . . not melodious song in all its lovely harmonies, not the sweet fragrance of flowers or ointments or spices, not manna or honey, not limbs that draw me to carnal embrace: none of these do I love when I love my God. And yet I do love a kind of light, a kind of voice, a certain fragrance, a food and an embrace, when I love my God: a light, voice, fragrance, food and embrace for my inmost self, where something limited to no place shines into my mind. . . . This is what I love, when I love God![9]

It is the "and yet" that turns me back to my own deepest need to see, to hear, to touch, to taste, to be embraced by the resurrected One. What does the resurrected One and his life look like, sound like, feel like? What would it be like if all our collective grief, all our sorrows, all our fears of death and terror were met head on in a single human life? It might look like a human figure stretching out arms to embrace all the world's pain, only to have those same arms enfold with undying love all that we are and all that we may yet be.

"Love is strong as death," so sings the Song of Solomon (8:6). "Goodness is stronger than evil," so sings Archbishop Tutu of South Africa.[10] Love is the truth that lives at the heart of resurrection.

What would a human life look like, sound like, feel like if it incarnated such truths? It might look like a community of people engaging all the rest of us with a hospitality that will not quit, with a respect that honors the least and the last. It might be a way of life that seeks the transformation of all that is creaturely: earth, air, water, light, bread, fruit of the vine, and all manner of human persons . . . "all creatures great and small."[11] It looks like the most humble giving and receiving: the cup of cold water, clothing around the body, the feeding of the children. It is the sound of "peace," "fear not," and that ultimate being known and cherished.

So we sing Psalm 118: "O give thanks to the LORD, for he is good; for his steadfast love endures forever!" So we shout with the great words of John on Patmos in Revelation: "The Alpha and the Omega, the beginning and the end" (Rev. 21:6). So we must live into the mystery of God forever with us . . . reversing the world's way of saying: death is death; what's real is what's real; what you see is what you get.

The great mystery is this: that the wounded healer allows us to touch, to hear, to taste, and to see—and bids us move in God's deep circling of grace. God comes to our senses with a reality that transfigures this life by what eye has not seen nor ear heard.

This is what the Resurrection *sounds* like . . .
This is what the Resurrection *tastes* like . . .
This is what the Resurrection *looks* like . . .

God remembers and embraces human life with a love and grace that death cannot undo, and *we are to be the witnesses.* As Christ was sent, so are we. Let us witness to the resurrection, even in the midst of suffering and difficulty, in every time and season, through all the rhythms of life. For Jesus Christ stretches forth his arms to embrace us and, through our witness, will win the world with love and mercy. Amen.[12]

—DON SALIERS

# RADIATING
# FAITH

# Breath of God Prayer

LOVING GOD, YOU HAVE BLESSED us with the gift of your Holy Spirit who breathes new life into us and all that we do. We have taken time out of our busy lives for the Academy and there found a space to celebrate the word you have given us in communal study, prayer, and silence. In that sacred space, you have entered our lives anew and called us closer to you and one another.

Now we ask you to continue to breathe your holy breath into us and into all the spaces and places where you call us to minister and live as your creation. We ask you confidently for you are the God who loves us unconditonally and wants us to experience your life to the fullest. In Jesus' name we pray. Amen.

—SR. KATHLEEN FLOOD, OP

# Open Heart Prayer

DEAR GOD, FATHER GOD, Mother God, God Eternal, Jesus the Begotten Son, Holy Spirit, Creator, Sustainer, Giver of Life; we have opened ourselves to new ideas, new ways of the Spirit, and a deepening of the soul. We recognize that the struggle to find vision for life in community is part of a process. But we must say, Lord, sometimes we are tempted to change the process instead of allowing it to happen.

When we are honest, we must say that sometimes we have been frightened, challenged, overwhelmed, and intimidated in discovering ourselves through this journey toward you, this journey of rhythm and fire.

Yet we open our hearts to you.

We pray that we will be able to live out the Spirit we have found in community and solitude. We trust that the outcome will be good for our hearts and for your world, yet even more deeply we trust that it will be pleasing to you.

So, our hearts have been exposed; our spirits have been challenged; our minds have been opened. Now we offer our lives back to you to be formed and shaped and even inflamed with your passionate love. In Christ's name. Amen.

—GLANDION CARNEY

# Elijah and the Cave

EARLY SUCCESS in ministry, no matter how dramatic, doesn't always ward off a sense of anxiety and dis-ease later on. Take the case of Elijah, the Old Testament prophet.

No one had a more spectacular beginning. Shocked at the king's apostasy, Elijah predicts a drought that lasts three years. Miraculously saved by the widow of Zarephath, he revives her son from death. Disgusted by the prophets of Baal, he summons the king, zaps the altar, and orders all those disgusting prophets of Baal killed. Pretty dramatic stuff. Then, as a *coup d'état*, he ends the drought with a little puff of a cloud.

Taunting, confident, full of bravado, Elijah is never depicted as acting on his own. He is instead Yahweh's servant, an obedient messenger. So why is Jezebel's threat (1 Kings 19:2) so unnerving? What does he have to fear from this floozy, who makes vows to false gods while covering for her pathetic husband, Ahab?

Yet Elijah is clearly terrified, and he flees for his life. Is there something about Jezebel that particularly brings him down? some shadow side in his subconscious that is thrown into conflict by this raw display of female power and her lust for violence? Good stuff for speculation! Whatever the triggers, Elijah's interior journey is just beginning. Discouraged and ready to die, he is fed by an angel who pushes him farther into the wilderness (angels sometimes do this). Loosed from all familiarity, on his own for forty days and forty nights, he comes to the mountain of God.

A lot can happen to someone in forty days and forty nights. The Bible's full of those stories: Noah on the boat, Moses on the mountain with God, Jesus in the wilderness. It's a magical number, a number that signifies personal transformation. My guess is that Elijah had to give up every single one of those early successes during those forty days and forty nights; every single assurance, every single ego-filled moment of supreme self-confidence. Perhaps he hopes that at the end of these days and nights he will die. Or God will forget about him. Or he can retire—draw out his prophet's pension and buy a condo on the Reed Sea. The cave where he ends up must feel like a perfect place to spend a few days until the storm passes.

But it does not pass. It intensifies. Wind, earthquake, and fire. None of these bring Elijah out of the cave until he hears something else—the sound of sheer silence. The silence forces him from his cave. And the silence sends him back into the messiness of being a prophet again, into the God-forsaken ministry of engaging the principalities and powers of evil set loose in Israel by Ahab and Jezebel.

I say God-forsaken because that's how it must have appeared to others. In truth, the Elijah we encounter *after* chapter 19 of First Kings is a different Elijah. He rests on a quiet confidence in the presence of God in pronouncing stunning prophecy after stunning prophecy. The sheer silence of God's presence did not silence Elijah. It seems to have given him an even more purified word to proclaim to a wayward people, a word that includes compassion (sparing Ahab because of his penance) and companionship as Elisha comes alongside. Let's not romanticize that "sheer silence" passage; it does not signal Elijah's withdrawal from the world or an end to the stinging message of judgment that he brings. But it does free him from whatever terrified him in Jezebel's threat, and he prophesies now without fear (see 2 Kings 1:15ff.).

Elijah's story stands as a paradigm for those who contributed to this book. All of the authors have either participated in the two-year Academy for Spiritual Formation or taught there. Lasting forty days and forty nights (where did we get that idea), the Academy includes sixteen courses that outline the major topics in Christian spirituality. The deeper journey is from the head to the heart, removing barriers of fear and isolation and inviting lonely leaders into spiritual community before kicking them out into the world again. Most of us are not in the teeth of the battle as Elijah was, but all of our battles are real and promise more fruit than we can imagine. At the end of the two years (there are eight quarterly five-day sessions), participants are invited to pick up Elijah's mantle to do "more than you can ask or imagine." Just like Elisha.

In my case, I was a well-educated, well-trained, well-adjusted pastor serving a wonderful, loving congregation when the hunger came for something more. I went to the Academy not knowing what I was looking for and in deep denial about my needs. The loneliness of parish ministry was consuming me; my faith was poorly formed, my ministry limited by an overdeveloped sense of caution. I needed healing in places I didn't know were broken, and I needed to repent in ways that I could only begin to understand. Bottom line, the Academy led me to a Christ I never knew, freed me to celebrate the Spirit's delightful presence, and gave me courage to claim my own gifts and calling. I am deeply grateful to Danny Morris and all of those who founded the Academy, the wonderful leadership team for my Academy (#7), and all those who continue to make it the authentic witness it is.

—JERRY P. HAAS

# Notes

## AWAKENING TO SACRED FIRE

1. Joan D. Chittister, *Wisdom Distilled from the Daily: Living the Rule of St. Benedict Today* (San Francisco: HarperSanFrancisco, 1991), 28.

2. Ibid., 27.

3. "Praying for Vision" by Minerva G. Carcaño, *A Book of Personal Prayer*, comp. René O. Bideaux (Nashville, TN: Upper Room Books, 1997), 124.

## LONGING AND WRESTLING

1. Jalal al-Din Rumi, "Love Dogs," *The Essential Rumi*, trans. Coleman Barks et al. (San Francisco: HarperSanFrancisco, 1995), 155.

2. Mother Teresa, *Come Be My Light: The Private Writings of the "Saint of Calcutta,"* ed. Brian Kolodiejchuk (New York: Doubleday, 2007), 223.

3. C. S. Lewis, *The Pilgrim's Regress: An Allegorical Apology for Christianity, Reason and Romanticism* (Grand Rapids, MI: William B. Eerdmans Publishing, 1992), 204.

4. The bare or "naked" intent is understood to the be very heart of prayer itself in the medieval mystical tract *The Cloud of Unknowing* and is the centerpiece of Father Thomas Keating's revival of an ancient form of contemplative, or "centering," prayer.

5. Rabindranath Tagore, *Gitanjali (Song Offerings): A Collection of Prose Translations Made by the Author from the Original Bengali* (New York: Macmillan Publishing Company, 1971), 115.

6. T. S. Eliot, "East Coker," in *Four Quartets* (San Diego: Harvest Book/Harcourt, 1971), 31.

7. "Little Gidding," in ibid., 59.

8. Joyce Rupp, *Praying Our Goodbyes* (Notre Dame, IN: Ave Maria Press, 1988), 76.

9. "Psalm 63, (In the Morning I Will Sing)," adapted by David Goodrich from the *Good News Bible, Upper Room Worshipbook: Music and Liturgies for Spiritual Formation*, comp. and ed. Elise S. Eslinger (Nashville, TN: Upper Room Books, 2006), 279.

10. Howard Thurman, *Meditations of the Heart* (1953; reprint, Richmond, IN: Friends United Press, 1976), 176.

11. *Upper Room Worshipbook*, no. 260.

12. *Upper Room Worshipbook*, no. 288.

13. "An Order for Evening Praise and Prayer," *The United Methodist Hymnal* (Nashville, TN: United Methodist Publishing House, 1989), 878.

14. See *The Proper for the Lesser Feasts and Fasts*, 2006 (New York: Church Publishing, 2006), 271.

15. Abba Poemen, quoted in *The Sayings of the Desert Fathers: The Alphabetical Collection*, rev. ed., trans. Benedicta Ward (Kalamazoo, MI: Cistercian Publications, 1984), 178.

16. Abba Arsenius, quoted in ibid., 10.

## LISTENING TO THE SILENCE

1. "Let All Mortal Flesh Keep Silence," *The United Methodist Hymnal* (Nashville, TN: The United Methodist Publishing House, 1989), no. 626.

2. Flora Slosson Wuellner, *Prayer, Stress, and Our Inner Wounds* (Nashville, TN: Upper Room Books, 1985), 78.

3. Thomas Keating, *Invitation to Love: The Way of Christian Contemplation* (Rockport, MA: Element, 1992), 90.

4. See Patricia Loring, *Spiritual Discernment: The Context and Goal of Clearness Committees* (Wallingford, PA: Pendle Hill Publications, 1992), 24.

5. Bideaux, *A Book of Personal Prayer*, 142–43.

6. "Psalm 131:1-2," *The Psalms: An Inclusive Language Version Based on the Grail Translation from the Hebrew* (Chicago: GIA Publications, Inc., 1993), 238.

7. This psalm is traditionally attributed to David, and this essay will presume upon this for simplicity of discussion.

8. Susan Gregg-Schroeder, *In the Shadow of God's Wings: Grace in the Midst of Depression* (Nashville, TN: Upper Room Books, 1997), 116.

9. W. A. Jurgens, trans., *The Faith of the Early Fathers*, vol. 3 (Collegeville, MN: Liturgical Press, 1979), 32.

10. Wendy Wright, Academy for Spiritual Formation lectures, Academy #12. Syracuse, Indiana, September 30–October 5, 1997.

11. Frederick Buechner, *Wishful Thinking: A Theological ABC* (New York: Harper and Row, Publishers, 1973), 95.

## MOVING TO THE RHYTHM OF GRACE

1. "Walking in the Light of God," *Upper Room Worshipbook* (Nashville, TN: Upper Room Books, 2006), no. 433.

2. Tilden Edwards, *Living in the Presence: Spiritual Exercises to Open Your Life to the Awareness of God* (San Francisco: Harper SanFrancisco, 1995), 18.

## LIVING COMMUNITY/LIVING FLAMES

1. *Upper Room Worshipbook*, 6–7.

2. Gregg-Schroeder, *In the Shadow of God's Wings*, 14.

3. From E. Glenn Hinson's participation in sessions with Thomas Merton at Merton's hermitage beginning in 1961.

4. Charles A. Reich, *The Greening of America* (New York: Random House, 1970), 233–85.

5. *The Confessions of St. Augustine*, trans. John K. Ryan (Garden City, NY: Image Books, 1960), 43.

6. George Herbert, "The Elixir," in *The Country Parson, The Temple*, ed. John N. Wall Jr. (New York: Paulist Press, 1981), 311.

7. Thomas H. Troeger, "These Things Did Thomas Count as Real," in *Borrowed Light: Hymn Texts, Prayers and Poems* (New York: Oxford University Press, 1994), 163.

8. Matthew Bridges, "Crown Him with Many Crowns," *The United Methodist Hymnal*, no. 327.

9. Saint Augustine, *The Confessions*, trans. Maria Boulding, ed. John E. Rotelle, pt. 1, vol. 1 of *The Works of Saint Augustine: A Translation for the Twenty-First Century* (Hyde Park, NY: New City Press, 1997), 242.

10. "Goodness Is Stronger Than Evil," *The Faith We Sing* (Nashville, TN: Abingdon Press, 2000), no. 2219.

11. Cecil Frances Alexander, "All Things Bright And Beautiful," *The United Methodist Hymnal*, no. 147.

12. Rev. Dr. Don E. Saliers' sermon for Pyoung chon Methodist Church, 1 June 2007.

# About the Academy for Spiritual Formation®

THE ACADEMY BEGAN in 1983 after five years of praying, planning, and preparing. Danny E. Morris, on the staff of The Upper Room in Nashville, sensed that people needed a place to go deeper in their faith, exploring the riches of Christian spirituality. Conversations with people like Morton Kelsey, Rueben Job, Flora Slosson Wuellner, Glenn Hinson, and others spurred on Danny's "nudge." He visited Saint Meinrad's Archabbey (Benedictine) in Indiana. A strong extrovert, he found the silence difficult but also knew that it could be fruitful. Gradually a design began to form in his mind and spirit. When he felt ready, he drew together an advisory council for discernment. John Mogabgab, then graduate assistant to Henri Nouwen at Yale, developed the course descriptions and recruited the faculty. The first Academy was held in Nashville, Tennessee, at the Scarritt-Bennett Center.

The two-year Academy consists of eight five-day sessions: a total of forty days. Participants gather every three months at the same location to experience a rhythm of spiritual community, which includes morning prayer, lecture, silence, Holy Communion, and small groups, followed by night prayer (Compline). This approach to spiritual formation emphasizes both head and heart. Additional elements, including a "wellness" component, create a holistic appreciation of body, mind, and spirit.

For more information about the Academy for Spiritual Formation go to www.upperroom.org/academy or contact:

JERRY HAAS, Academy for Spiritual Formation
P.O. Box 340004,
Nashville, TN 37203-0004.
Phone 1-877-899-2781, ext. 7233
Email: academy@upperroom.org

# About the Contributors

*All of the contributors to this volume have either participated in a two-year Academy (indicated by the number [#] of their Academy) or served as faculty (fac.) for the Academy for Spiritual Formation. The letters* UMC *indicate the United Methodist Church.*

Chris Bahnson (#22) serves as Coordinator of Caring Ministries at St. Mark's UMC in Tucson, Arizona. Her focus is mentoring people in spiritual gifts, prayer ministry, and compassionate care.

Robert Benson (#6 and fac.) is a freelance writer, living in Nashville, Tennessee. His book *Living Prayer* (Tarcher/Putnam, 1998) tells the story of his journey through the Academy for Spiritual Formation.

René O. Bideaux (#4) has served as a local church pastor (UM), missionary, denominational executive and retreat leader in spiritual formation. His prayer was first published in a book he edited: *A Book of Personal Prayer* (Nashville, TN: Upper Room Books, 1997).

Roberta Bondi (fac.) is an early church history scholar, recently retired from Candler School of Theology, Emory University, Atlanta. Her rich encounters with the desert fathers and mothers shaped her numerous writings and her life.

Minerva G. Carcaño (fac.) is the bishop for the Phoenix Area of the UMC and is passionate about spiritual formation and social justice. A native of Texas, she credits much of her early spiritual formation to her grandmother Sophia.

Glandion Carney (#25 and fac.) is a teacher, spiritual director, and author, living in Birmingham, Alabama.

Robert Carr (#12) is a Disciples of Christ pastor in the Kansas City area. He often leads workshops on Centering Prayer.

Nancy Bryan Crouch (#4) is the publisher for the Order of St. Luke, an organization dedicated to liturgical renewal. An Episcopal layperson, she has served as Worship and Music Coordinator on several Academy leadership teams.

Linda Douty (#8 and fac.) is a spiritual director and author, living in Memphis, Tennessee. Her most recent book, *How Can I See the Light When It's So Dark,* was published by Morehouse (2007).

Elise S. Eslinger (fac.) has been actively involved in shaping the musical and liturgical life of the Academy from its beginning in 1983. She edited both the first (1985) and second (2006) *Worshipbooks* published by Upper Room Books.

Nancy Finlayson (#26) is an ordained pastor in the United Church of Canada, currently living in Winnipeg, Ontario.

Sr. Kathleen Flood, OP, (fac.) is member of the Sinsinawa Dominicans. She serves as director of Stillpoint in Nashville, a ministry of contemplation and spiritual direction.

Stephanie Ford (fac.) teaches at Earlham School of Religion in Richmond, Indiana, Society of Friends (Quaker) seminary. Ordained in the Baptist tradition, she completed her doctoral work on Evelyn Underhill, an Anglican.

Susan Gregg-Schroeder (#7) writes, teaches, and advocates through the organization she founded, Mental Health Ministries. Her book *In the Shadow of God's Wings* (Upper Room Books, 1997) describes her experience of faith while dealing with severe depression.
Web site: www.mentalhealthministries.net

Jerry P. Haas (#7) is Director of the Academy for Spiritual Formation and Emerging Ministries at the Upper Room. A native of South Dakota, he pastored churches in Arizona for twenty-five years before moving to Nashville.

Randall R. Hansen (#26) was a missionary in Uruguay and now pastors a UM church in Muskegon, Michigan.

Wil Hernandez (#19) is a writer, teacher, and spiritual director in Southern California. He is the author of *Henri Nouwen: A Spirituality of Imperfection* (Paulist Press, 2006).

E. Glenn Hinson (fac.) is well-recognized as a leader in spiritual formation in the Baptist tradition. He is a scholar, author, mentor, teacher, and spiritual guide, living in Louisville, Kentucky.

Judy Holloway (#11) teaches music in Graham, Texas. Judy has served as Worship and Music Coordinator on several two-year Academy teams.

Jo Hoover (#18) is a spiritual director and a retired United Methodist pastor in the Iowa Conference.

Ginger Howl (#7) lives in Stillwater, Oklahoma. She has served as Worship and Music Coordinator for many Academy teams.

Melanie Dobson Hughes (#24) studies healing and spiritual practices as part of her doctoral work at Duke University.

In-Sook Hwang (#18) is pastor of Pana United Methodist Church in Illinois. She is actively involved in Academy leadership, both for Korean- and English-speaking participants.

Sonja Ingebritsen (#24) is a United Church of Christ layperson, studying at Pacific School of Religion in Berkeley, California.

Hee-Soo Jung (#18 and fac.) is bishop of the Chicago Area United Methodist Church. A native of Korea, he converted to Christianity as a young man but continued to study Confucianism and Buddhism.

Marion Jackson (#18) is a United Methodist pastor in New Jersey and also an artist and poet.

Rueben P. Job (fac.) has influenced many through his writings and guidebooks on prayer. A retired United Methodist bishop, he served as World Editor of The Upper Room. His support helped Danny Morris create the Academy for Spiritual Formation, which was launched on May 17, 1983. He lives in Brentwood, Tennessee.

Linda and Billy Keen (#17) are Academy leaders in San Antonio, Texas, where Billy works as an artist and Linda works for the UMC in leadership formation. View Billy's work at www.billykeenart.com.

Cynthia Langston Kirk (#21) is a poet and liturgical artist with a ministry called Piecing Stories. She has written for *Living the Questions* and served as guest editor of *Alive Now*.

Regina Laroche (#18) is an African-Caribbean-American storyteller and dancer. She lives on Madeline Island in Lake Superior with her husband, Jeff Thuene, their two sons, and their dog, Kaia.

Kyunglim Shin Lee (#21) serves as Vice President of Wesley Theological Seminary in Washington DC. Her responsibilities for creating global centers and a global perspective on theological education highlight one of the top priorities of the seminary.

Hazelyn McComas (fac.) has taught at more than twenty-five Academies (two-year and five day). She traces her love of scripture back to her grandfather who was a Dutch Reformed pastor. She lives in Milwaukee, Wisconsin.

Cathie McFadden (#25) is a curriculum writer and workshop leader. She lives in the mountains of North Carolina with her husband and enjoys the outdoors.

Denise McGuiness (#24) is a psychologist in Oregon. She is active in retreat leadership and spiritual direction.

Sr. Dawn Annette Mills, OSB, (fac.) is a member of the Benedictine Sisters of Perpetual Adoration, located in Clyde, Missouri. She has written a book titled *The Gospel According to Dawn.*

Bob Mitchell (#10) is a pastor in Phoenix, Arizona. He recently completed his doctorate at Claremont School of Theology in Claremont, California.

R. Sidwell Mokgothu (fac.) is an ordained Methodist minister, currently working for the South African government. He advocates for Sedibeng, a South African adaptation of the Academy. This lament was written after his brother's suicide in 2003.

Lora Moore (#22) is a gardener, poet, and mentor in the faith. She and her husband, Carroll, live in New Hampshire.

Lynda Joan Morley (#21) is a contemplative, a lifelong learner, and a teacher. She prefers moving to the pace of *lectio divina* and enjoys facilitating groups with the Companions in Christ series. She lives in Nashville, Tennessee.

Robert C. Morris (fac.) is Executive Director of Interweave, a center for spirituality and life in Summit, New Jersey. Ordained in the Episcopal Church, Bob has published two books with Upper Room Books: *Wrestling with Grace* and *Provocative Grace* (2006).

Robert Mulholland (fac.) teaches at Asbury Theological Seminary in Wilmore, Kentucky. He delivered the first lectures at the first Academy for Spiritual Formation in 1983. The lectures became the basis for the book *Shaped by the Word* (Upper Room Books, revised edition, 2000).

Larry Peacock (#3 and fac.) directs Rolling Ridge Retreat Center in North Andover, Massachusetts. A spiritual director and retreat leader, Larry authored *Openings: A Daybook of Saints, Songs, and Prayers* (Upper Room Books, 2003).

Don Saliers (fac.) is a teacher, author, musician, theologian, and liturgical scholar. A part of the original Academy Advisory Board, he taught at Candler School of Theology (Emory University) in Atlanta for more than twenty years.

Suzanne Seaton (#5) is a spiritual director in the Seattle area, an active Academy leader and author of the book *Pilgrimage of the Soul: Thresholds to the Mystery* (with Sally M. O'Neil; published by Soaring Eagle, 2004).

Jan Sechrist (#24) is a UM layperson. She facilitates a contemplative worship service at her home church in northern California.

Luther E. Smith Jr. (fac.) teaches at Candler School of Theology (Emory University) in Atlanta. An expert on the life and writings of Howard Thurman, he serves as a member of the *Weavings* journal advisory board.

Linda Tatum (#20) taught English and worked in human resources. She and her husband, Barnes, live in Greensboro, North Carolina.

Marjorie J. Thompson (fac.) is an ordained minister in the Presbyterian Church (USA). A member of The Upper Room staff, she has authored and edited numerous books in the Companions in Christ series.

Jeanne Varnell (#1) is a spiritual director and community leader from Memphis, Tennessee. She has been a leader in supporting and developing the Academy.

Jane Vennard (fac.) is an ordained minister in the United Church of Christ. She serves as a spiritual director, teacher and author and lives in Denver, Colorado.

Cathy Warner (#24) lives in the Santa Cruz Mountains in northern California. She serves as a lay minister to a UM congregation, writes short stories and poetry, and leads workshops on writing as a spiritual practice.

Barbara Wendland (#1) writes a monthly newsletter, *Connections,* as a way to stimulate thinking and open the church to dialogue about matters of importance. She and her husband, Errol, live in Temple, Texas.

Wendy Wright (fac.) is an author, cantor, teacher, and spiritual director. She teaches at Creighton University and serves on the Advisory Board of the Academy for Spiritual Formation. She lives in Omaha, Nebraska.

This page is an extension of the copyright page.

*The publisher gratefully acknowledges permissions to reproduce the following copyrighted material:*

*About the cover art*

Dr. He Qi's bold and captivating artwork tells the story of Elijah being taken up to heaven. Elijah stands with hands wide open to the hovering angel. The chariot's wheel is a sign of our journey with God, and the fire indicates the Spirit's transforming power, ready to be launched on a dreary world. Elisha waits and watches with hands cupped in prayer. His face suggests the awesome authority he has been asked to assume (2 Kings 2).